SPARTNERS

Discover the Value in Your Spouse as a Business Partner and Enrich Your Marriage

BY
Troy & Shantel Brooks

SPARTNERS
Discover the Value in Your Spouse as a Business Partner and Enrich Your Marriage.
Copyright © 2024 by Troy and Shantel Brooks.

All rights reserved. No part of this publication may be reproduced, distributed, or transmitted in any form or by any means, including photocopying, recording, or other electronic or mechanical methods, or any information storage and retrieval system, without the prior written permission of the author or publisher, except in the case of brief quotations embodied in critical reviews and certain other commercial uses permitted by copyright law. For permission requests, write to the publisher at Info@thetbeffect.com

Library of Congress Control Number: 2024905655
Paperback ISBN: 979-8-9902800-1-4
Hardback ISBN: 979-8-9902800-2-1
Cover art by ThriveIn Learning LLC
Edited by Naomi Books, LLC
Published by TB Effect Press
Printed in the United States of America

The names and experiences of contributors to this book are used with their permission.

Scripture references herein are taken from the Bible versions as listed below:

English Standard Version (ESV): Scripture quotations are from The ESV® Bible (The Holy Bible, English Standard Version®), © 2001 by Crossway, a publishing ministry of Good News Publishers. Used by permission. All rights reserved.

New King James Version (NKJV): Scripture taken from the New King James Version®. Copyright © 1982 by Thomas Nelson. Used by permission. All rights reserved.

New Living Translation (NLT): *Holy Bible*, New Living Translation, copyright © 1996, 2004, 2015 by Tyndale House Foundation. Used by permission of Tyndale House Publishers, Inc., Carol Stream, Illinois 60188. All rights reserved.

New International Version (NIV): Holy Bible, New International Version®, NIV® Copyright ©1973, 1978, 1984, 2011 by Biblica, Inc.® Used by permission. All rights reserved worldwide.

SPARTNERS (noun)

[spart-ners]

Spouses who are business partners.

But seek first his kingdom and His righteousness, and all these things will be given to you as well.

—Matthew 6:33 NIV

CONTENTS

Dedications 1
In Memory 3
Introduction 5
CHAPTER ONE: Marriage is Tough 11
CHAPTER TWO: A Marriage and Business Partnership Can Thrive 33
CHAPTER THREE: Guess What? You Married on Purpose! 53
CHAPTER FOUR: You Are Built for This 71
CHAPTER FIVE: Iron Sharpens Iron 85
CHAPTER SIX: Let Go; It's Okay 101
CHAPTER SEVEN: Lean In 117
CHAPTER EIGHT: Reach Your Goals, Together! 129
CHAPTER NINE: So, How Would This Work? 147
CHAPTER TEN: *Spartner*s = Priceless 169
CHAPTER ELEVEN: Becoming Spartners 177
About the Authors 181
References 183

DEDICATIONS

To our Heavenly Father:
We give you all the praise. May this work glorify your Kingdom.

To our beloved children, Sage and Phoenix:
You are our miracles and blessings who fuel us each day. May you always know how much you are loved and strengthened through Christ and your papa and mama.

To our parents:
We love you and appreciate all your unwavering support, encouragement, protection, and love.

To our spiritual family, Change Church:
Thank you for guiding us toward our encounter with Christ, planting the roots of our marriage ministry, and giving us the platform to spread His message.

To future and current Spartners:
May you grow closer to God each day, thus closer and closer to one another, truly becoming one.

IN MEMORY

In loving memory of *Shavonne Latoya Johnson*.

May we all have the softened heart and forgiving spirit she carried each day.

INTRODUCTION

There are many reasons why people get married today. People may marry because it makes sense financially; it is expected of them culturally; a baby is on the way; they don't want to be alone; or for some crazy people, because they really love each other. That's us! We love each other to the moon and back—forever and always—and all that other lovey-dovey stuff that may make you want to roll your eyes and possibly even close this book.

If you are like us, you married your spouse (or plan to marry your partner) because you love them more deeply than their pockets, beyond their appearance, and above all the other things society deems "marriage worthy." Your faith binds you, and your commitment to each other is unbreakable. Your loyalty to one another is unmeasurable. If this is you... this book is FOR YOU!

We wrote this book for spouses who love each other, trust each other, and want to live a quality life with each other, hand in hand. You believe God has intentionally brought you together to become one. You think about your spouse, and you smile as you reflect on how you first met and who got whose number first (or Instagram handle, email, online dating approval, TikTok, etc.).

As you think about what you admire in your spouse, your heart fills with joy and warmth. When you sit back and reminisce about how you've supported each other, you can't help but get teary-eyed (or close to it). We wrote this book for those spouses who, despite the temptation, negative perceptions, naysayers, and tough work, have chosen to marry each other and commit themselves to each other every day for the rest of their lives.

INTRODUCTION

When you think about your spouse, the amount of time you may spend with them, and the quality of time you spend with them, you may notice that you don't have as much *control* over your lives as you may have thought. You may unknowingly work against each other with conflicting schedules/priorities set outside your control, and you really only know who they are in part.

If you and your spouse have two separate careers/jobs, your schedules are likely filled with your individual tasks, and there is too little time shared between the two of you. With that also comes limited experiences you can partake in, extra stress, and less quality time you can enjoy together. Sometimes, your schedules and priorities may conflict, which can cause a divide between the two of you and lead to unnecessary conflict and tension in your marriage. Even though you support each other's individual goals, purposes, and dreams, these individual pursuits may require a sacrifice of energy, effort, and time that you could be spending together.

You may also notice that you only really know one dimension or one side of your spouse. This may become clearer when you join them at a work function and see how assertive or withdrawn they appear, but you know them to be the complete opposite at home. When you hang out with their friends, you may notice they are more outgoing and talkative or quiet and reserved. Also, when you have a child, the spouse you came to know (or the *part* of them you fell in love with) can also transform into a version that is new.

You and your spouse have multiple strengths, multiple ways to love, and multiple ways to show up in various situations and environments. When you only spend nights and maybe weekends with your spouse, you miss out on *all* of who they are and potentially who they are becoming.

We wrote this book to give married couples an alternate way to elevate their marriage by discovering the value in their spouse as a business partner. Neither of you need to be an entrepreneur to make this happen, nor do you need to quit your job. You only need to:

1. Be in a healthy marriage;
2. Be ready to move your marriage from good to great;
3. Be open to the idea of working with your spouse; and
4. Be committed to the strategies and practices we share in this book.

If you meet the four conditions above, allow this book to help you discover the value in your spouse being your business partner to enrich and elevate your marriage.

Knowing the value of your marriage is essential to ensuring it remains a priority in your life. To know the value of your marriage, you need to recognize the value of your spouse, and even deeper, your own value. To do this, we encourage you to first learn the value God has placed on you. Psalm 139:14 (NKJV) says, "I will praise You, for I am fearfully *and* wonderfully made; Marvelous are Your works, And *that* my soul knows very well."

God made us in *His* image—He made us perfect for His way. We are His temple, and His Spirit resides in us. So, if you feel unseen or undervalued, remember this—you were wonderfully made! You *can* have greatness! You *can* have respect. And you most certainly *can* have love.

You cannot really know the value of your marriage if you are struggling with owning your *own* value. Recognizing your *own* worth is a foundational step to building a healthy and fulfilling relationship with your spouse.

Discovering the value in your spouse for your marriage is pivotal for a thriving relationship. Here's why it's so crucial:

- There is Connection and Intimacy:
  When you appreciate your partner's value, it strengthens the emotional connection between you. It creates a sense of intimacy, fostering a deeper understanding and closeness in your relationship.

INTRODUCTION

- There is Mutual Respect:
  Recognizing your partner's value demonstrates respect for their individuality, strengths, and contributions. It builds a foundation of mutual respect,atch is fundamental for a strong and lasting relationship.

- There are Positive Dynamics:
  Recognizing each other's value creates a more positive atmosphere. It leads to a supportive environment where both partners feel validated and encouraged in their endeavors.

Let's make a conscious effort to discover the value in our spouses as business partners.

When you run a business with your spouse, there are skills needed, personalities required, and trust established to make it work. You will learn how to navigate challenges in strategic ways you may not have explored before. You'll experience compassion and patience, as well as appreciation and gratitude, which are revealed when working with your spouse. Becoming a business partner with your spouse can help elevate your marriage because of the unique demands and challenges it presents to your marriage. If you can work together through these external pressures, your marriage can sprout to heights of connectedness, love, and joy that could have otherwise taken years to reach, if ever.

We invite you to consider and explore the value within your spouse as a business partner as you read our personal stories. They demonstrate strength, hardship, love, and conflict as we found our way to each other, as *Spartners*, and watched our marriage thrive. If you're already *Spartners*, please allow this book to guide you into reflecting on *how* you value your spouse in marriage and business, and exploring ways in which you both can value each other more.

Throughout this book, we will give you tools and scriptures to apply to your marriage and *Spartner*ship (marriage + business). We will share interesting research, as well as suggestions and lessons about what worked for us. You'll also learn from other *Spartners'* experiences. At the end of each chapter, you will find concrete practices or mindset shifts to help you discover value in your spouse as a business partner.

A deeper dive into the layout of this book is as follows:

- Chapters 1 and 2 address "the elephant in the room" (Marriage is Tough) and the truth untold (A Marriage and Business Partnership *Can* Thrive).
- Chapters 3 through 7 help you uncover beliefs and ideas that may be holding you back from truly seeing value within your spouse.
- Chapters 8 through 11 help show you what working with your spouse can actually look like if you "Let Go" and "Lean In."

There are many strategies you can use to elevate your marriage, but very few options for frameworks. Becoming *Spartners* (spouses who are business partners), is a framework that will certainly stretch you, refine you, and reveal things to you. It can also enhance your marriage in a way very few things can, thus bringing your marriage, and possibly your professional ambition, to heights never imagined.

> *Whatever you have learned or received or heard from me, or seen in me—put it into practice. And the God of peace will be with you.*
>
> —PHILIPPIANS 4:9 NIV

CHAPTER ONE
Marriage is Tough

"I just need you to listen."

"You're not letting me finish!"

"You always do that, but when I do it, it's a problem."

"I have three kids—our two children and you!"

"That's how you choose to spend your time. That's not my problem."

"That's not what we agreed on."

"Your failure to plan is not my emergency."

"Well, then *you* do it!"

"Your bra has been sitting on this dresser for four days. You've had to open your drawer and close it several times. Why can't you just put it back in the drawer?"

"They are *your* parents."

"Why can't you just place the dish in the dishwasher... not the sink?"

"I love how you move the goalpost when it suits you."

"You spent how much?"

"I need you to understand."

"Talk to me when you're not in your ego."

Is there ever a day when one of these comments—or something similar—isn't made? We love each other, of course, but marriage is a dance where the music does not end. The song may change, the rhythm will certainly vary, and sometimes even the lyrics are spoken in languages not understood. In any dance intended to last forever, it is only natural for one partner to sit out and take a break while their partner keeps the vibrations going. Soon enough, that partner may slide back in and give their partner a chance to do the same. Sometimes a partner doesn't even know they need a break until their ankle gives out or until they are told to just be still. There are times, in any dance which lasts forever, when it is only natural that the groove and the connection are so *on point* that both partners get lost in the melody. They allow time to pass by without even checking for it. It is also only natural for these two partners to bump heads, lose the beat, step on each other's toes, or both want to quit at the same time. Marriage is a dance... a long, forever dance that can be so beautiful, yet so tough.

> **Marriage can be the toughest partnership you will ever endure**

With a title like *Spartners,* you probably thought we would start by saying "marriage is the best choice you can make" or "our marriage is the best," or even "get married and change your life!" While those statements can be true on any given day, that is not our message.

Marriage can be the toughest partnership you will ever endure if you decide to jump the broom and commit your life, spirit, and body to someone else. Marriage can not only be tough because you're legally and financially responsible for each other, but also for a slew of other reasons.

> *But if you do marry, you have not sinned; and if a virgin marries, she has not sinned. But those who marry will face many troubles in this life, and I want to spare you this.*
> —1 CORINTHIANS 7:28 NIV

SPARTNERS

*****

You can be spread thin and not have time for yourself.

Troy's Story: Sacrifices

I flew into Atlanta to get our new house in order days before Shantel (who was more than eight months pregnant) planned to come with Sage (our then two-and-a-half-year-old). I never stopped organizing, putting things away, and getting stuff together while I was there. I continued to get our home in order because we decided to have a home birth immediately after getting to Atlanta. Once my five-day trip was up, I drove thirteen hours back to New York to get Shantel and Sage, as they were staying in a hotel after a family COVID-19 scare. I had devoted all my time to ensuring everything was as great as it could be prior to their arrival. After I arrived to pick them up, we immediately turned back around and went to our new home.

With my mind so focused on the house, I could not find the energy to work out at all, and this was an essential part of my life. Because everything fell into my hands, not to mention just trying to parent and learn about our new surroundings, I felt spread thin. I wasn't angry about it. I actually found much gratitude in being able to take it all on, but I had to sacrifice my body, and I have yet to really get it back.

Shantel's Story: I Can Do It!

I take on a lot all the time, and as a result, I sign up to do more than I should. I don't know my bandwidth, and I'm always overly confident that I can do it all. Somehow, I do it *all* and can handle it, but I rarely find time for myself. I then complain, "There's no time for me." I'll say, "I didn't get to talk to my friends on the phone today" or "I need a nap." Sometimes it's "I just need to take a shower!" Without realizing I do this to myself, I often find myself saying, "Yes, I'll do it," and then catch myself complaining about it later. No one forces me to take on everything I do. I am just your typical over-achiever who *enjoys* it... until I don't. Then, I am smelly, tired, and annoyed that I have no time for *me*.

Our Story: Not Every Night Needs to be Date Night.

Shared by Shantel

At times, a partner can feel like they are literally giving all of themselves to everybody and everything around them, and not giving anything to themselves. Certainly, there are days when all our energy is first put into our children, followed by getting the house in order, our work projects, and, if fortunate, each other—*if* there is time.

There are nights when we both feel exhausted, like we just need a minute to be by ourselves. We may go into separate rooms or even sit side by side in silence, doing our own thing. A great friend once told us, "Not every night needs to be date night." This could not be truer. As *Spartners*, parents, and just people... we need time for ourselves. It's essential.

> **As *Spartners*, parents, and just people... we need time for ourselves. It's essential.**

> *Don't worry about anything; instead, pray about everything. Tell God what you need, and thank him for all he has done.*
>
> —PHILIPPIANS 4:6 NLT

Our Thoughts

Marriage requires a lot from each partner, and even more when there are children involved. There are needs that parallel each other and there are needs that conflict. There are demands that are warranted and there are demands that partners put on each other based on their own experiences. A constant push and pull exists and seems never to go away. There are seasons of happiness and possibly seasons of despair.

There are moments in marriage when each partner can feel spread extremely thin. With each added layer of finances, children, illness, etc., the tension, pressure, and stress can become more intense and unmanageable. Taking time for each of you is critical if you are going to be fruitful for each other. As the saying goes, "You can't pour into the cups of others if your cup is empty." Of course, having a full cup every day isn't realistic (if we're being honest), but having *something* in your cup is totally possible and necessary. When this is not the case, and your cup is empty, resentment can arise, along with sheer exhaustion and strife within the relationship.

Marriage can be tough.

Contrary to what many believe, the leading cause of divorce in 2023 was a lack of commitment to the union.

Revealing Divorce Statistics In 2024

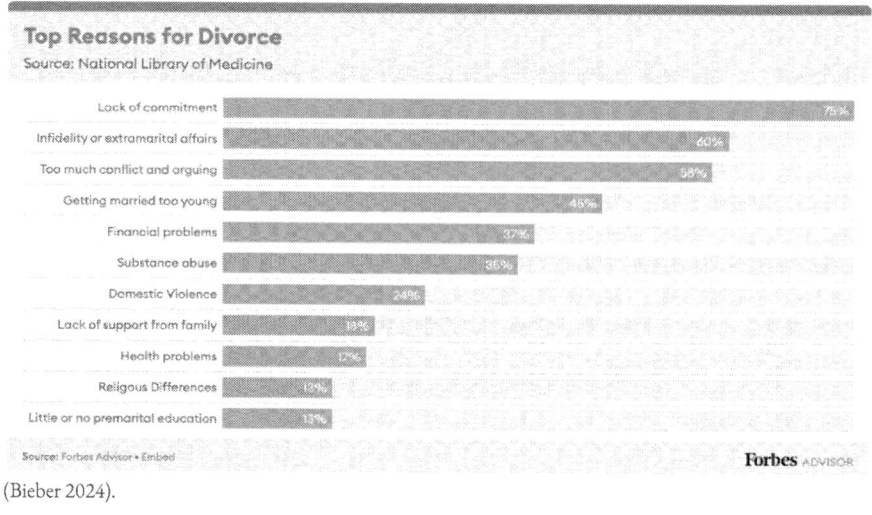

(Bieber 2024).

* * * * *

You can grow apart... grow incompatible.

Our Story: The Avid Runner and the Social Butterfly.

Shared by Troy

Shantel scouted me before asking me to train her. (We dive deeper into our story in the next chapter.) She saw I was a Believer, partygoer, foodie, attractive, and loved to work out. From the beginning, we shared the same interests, similar hobbies, and a similar taste for living life. Over the course of our marriage, we've each shown interest in new things the other is not crazy about (e.g., Game of Thrones or going dairy free). For the most part, however, we work intentionally to show interest in what the other finds of value. This helps strengthen our bond as a couple and enables us to evolve as individuals.

Shantel became very invested in equity and inclusion within the education space. She would come home daily and talk about her learnings and actions. I heard the passion in her voice. I also saw the overlap in the fitness world and began to share the excitement of the new learning with her. She was also a runner and began training for races. Although I liked to run, it was typically three to six miles, and I never ran with the intention of getting into races. Shantel enjoyed my company when I joined her. Soon, we began to train for our first (and only) half marathon together. It was an achievement we celebrated together.

I always had an infatuation with watches. Shantel never cared much about watches, but to support my passion, she would go to dealers with me and watch YouTube reviews about the watches I appreciated most. I'm also very personable, always connecting with people and attending events, art shows, and new experiences. Shantel is more reserved, but stepped out of her comfort zone and accompanied me everywhere I went. She has since fallen in love with adventure and spontaneity.

At any moment, we could have each gone our own way. Shantel, the avid runner; me, the social butterfly. Instead, we choose to value each other and our passions and grow closer, rather than apart.

> *I pray that your love will overflow more and more, and that you will keep on growing in knowledge and understanding. For I want you to understand what really matters, so that you may live pure and blameless lives until the day of Christ's return.*
>
> —PHILIPPIANS 1:9-10 NLT

Our Thoughts

Marriage can pull partners onto two separate roads where they work in silos, away from each other. They can share the same house, same bathroom, and the same bed, yet be in two separate worlds. One spouse can find worth and value in self-transformation, working diligently to transform their life, perhaps taking part in wellness routines and rituals. The other may find worth and meaning by doing what they've always done: provide for the family and show up. One person can be a social butterfly, always wanting to be out and about, meeting new people, keeping old relationships alive, and just wanting to feel free. Their spouse may prefer to be a homebody, watch TV, have a good meal, and simply relax at home at the end of the day.

One person can prioritize their wellness to feel more connected to self and energized, while the other person may continue an unhealthy lifestyle that conflicts with that of their spouse. One partner may find joy in playing video games or scrolling through social media nonstop, while the other finds comfort in talking with colleagues who listen and give them attention. One spouse may devote all their energy to raising their children and being a great parent; while the other spouse seems less engaged, waiting to be seen or loved as they once felt they were (before parenthood). One spouse may choose to align with their family values and traditions, while the other just wants to build their own.

While experiencing these behaviors in isolation can be accepted within a marriage, if done subconsciously or not in alignment with your partner, problems can occur.

There are so many ways spouses can grow apart. It takes awareness, effort, communication, and compromise to work through a lot of the growing pains experienced in a marriage. If we continue to think about marriage as a dance, we know that for the dance to look beautiful, both dancers (spouses) must dance to the same song, and even better, the same beat. (Those who don't have rhythm get a pass with this analogy, but you get the gist.) Most likely, you once shared the same interests, faith, and even watched the same shows. Over time, though, as you evolved and experiences occurred, those interests, and even the shows you watch, may have drastically changed. In some cases, your faith may have changed as well. That's when you realize you've grown apart and may no longer be compatible. If this occurs, without intervention, the doorway to infidelity and other troubles can get wider and wider.

Marriage can be tough.

*****

Your actions affect more than just you.

Our Story: Keep Some of You for You.

Shared by Troy

Your actions no longer only impact you, they also affect your spouse, and for that reason, marriage can be tough. It can be especially tough if you are or have married a free-spirited person who doesn't like to answer to anyone, be questioned by anyone, or be cornered. This is exactly who I am. While I enjoyed long-term relationships, I was never one to be controlled, and therefore enjoyed the freedom to do as I wished. I was okay putting others first, considering my partner's feelings, and was even mindful of how my actions affected the person I was with. However, if I ever felt as if I *had* to do or was *supposed* to do something a certain way, without coming to that idea myself, I would typically get defensive. I felt like it was an *attack* on my freedom.

Shantel rarely told me what to do, but she would often remind me about keeping some things private—just between us. I was always an "open book" and found value in sharing what I was experiencing with others. At the time, Shantel didn't "get it" and preferred to keep to herself. It took several conversations, arguments, and rolling of the eyes before I realized I needed to adjust some of what I shared with the public. Although these actions had nothing to do with Shantel, they still affected her. If I had been single, I would have told my partner to accept it or leave. As a married man, I knew the importance of us being on the same page. I had to consider my wife's feelings.

> *Yes, each of us will give a personal account to God. So let's stop condemning each other. Decide instead to live in such a way that you will not cause another believer to stumble and fall.*
>
> —ROMANS 14:12-13 NLT

Our Thoughts

Unlike being single when you can do your own thing, be out until you feel like going home; reheat leftovers you never want anyone to witness you eat; spend money ridiculously on getting your hair and nails done; or simply just sleep all day—once you're married, you have to consider your spouse and their feelings, time, needs, dietary restrictions, physical space, schedule—the list goes on! The *you* who was once free to roam, sleep, eat, burp, fart, work long hours, work no hours, spend every weekend with your parents, spend every night with friends, and everything in between, now has a partner to consider. While it may still be okay within your marriage to do these things, everything should be discussed and possibly negotiated with your spouse to maintain a healthy relationship.

Marriage can be tough.

* * * * *

You should resolve your conflicts.

> *What causes quarrels and what causes fights among you?*
> *Is it not this, that your passions are at war within you? You*
> *desire and do not have, so you murder.*
> *You covet and cannot obtain, so you fight and quarrel.*
> *You do not have, because you do not ask.*
> —JAMES 4:1-2 ESV

Our Story: No New Single Friends

Shared by Shantel

Conflicts in marriage are inevitable, natural, and necessary. During our time together (dating and married), we experienced and overcame conflicts that were essential in launching us into the next season of harvest and success. We saw that each conflict prepared us—almost armed us—for the bigger challenge that was ahead.

My dad always said, "Married people should only have married friends." I thought this was an old-school mentality, but also recognized the value and importance of limiting your circle to married people once married, as the minds and behaviors of singles are different. Not bad, not good, just different from that of a married person. Troy had heard this saying from my dad, too, and found value in it. Together, we would continue building with our single friends from our past, as they held special places in our hearts, but we were not interested in befriending new single people. We held an unspoken mantra, "no new friends" (in Drake's voice).

Years went by and this "no new *single* friends" mantra never came up since most of the new friends we made were married. One night, however, I went out and made a new friend—a new *single* friend. We talked, exchanged numbers, and made plans to connect again. When I got home, I was excited to tell Troy all about my new friend. His first question to me was, "Is she married?"

"Is she married?" Troy repeated.

"Umm, I don't think so… I mean, I didn't look at her hand. Umm… she didn't mention anything about a spouse… but I *do* know she lives…" I began to share what I had learned about this new single friend.

"So, she's not married?" Troy inquired, more coldly this time.

"No, I guess not… but what's the problem? We probably won't even speak again," I replied, remembering our once agreed-upon understanding.

"Shantel, we're not supposed to start having single friends," Troy said. "I thought you and I were on the same page about this. Their heads are just in different places, and we don't need that. It is my job to protect this marriage, and I don't love the idea of you hanging out with a new single friend."

He explained, "I'm sure she's great, but I'm also sure she's in a different place mentally. Naturally, she will invite you out and potentially put you in a predicament you don't need to experience. And when we do things with friends, it should be with other married *faithful* friends, unless they've been in our lives and truly respect our union... like we agreed. We have goals and dreams and don't need to put potential distractions on our path; we don't need the drama, especially if it's avoidable."

"There are married people who can be just as dangerous, if not more so, than single people," I argued.

"Yes, you're absolutely right. But the likelihood of a married friend putting you into spaces that do not serve you or **our** marriage is less likely than that of a single friend. I thought you believed this!" Troy said, defeated.

The truth was, I *did* believe it. Yes, of course, new *single* friends could end up being best friends, but they could also unintentionally *not* best serve our marriage.

"You're right, Troy," I conceded. "I didn't even think of it, but you're right."

That new single friend never texted or called me after that first exchange, and I didn't contact her either.

This conflict and conversation needed to happen for our marriage, as it re-centered our vision, dusted off our shared foundational values, and forced us to talk through a disagreement. Ironically, it also pushed us into our joint purpose of conviction to revitalize and rebrand marriage. From there, we created *Spartners*.

Do we love our single friends out there? Of course! Will we build with them at an event, in a park, or passing by? For sure! But will they become our new BFFs? Not if we don't share the same values, think similarly, or value marriage. This conflict needed to happen, as do many.

Marriage can be tough.

> **DID YOU KNOW?**
>
> "Scholars have suggested that conflict promotes well-being. Disagreement can enhance mental health and social adjustment insofar as it provides opportunities for improving self-expression and refining interpersonal collaboration skills" (Laursen and Hafen 2010).

Our Thoughts

When conflict occurs, you should work it out. Yes, some may go to bed angry, leave for a few nights, or even book a ticket for a quick trip (we definitely do *not* recommend that). Yet, at some point, the argument, conflict, disagreement, conversation (or whatever you want to call it) must be had, discussed, and resolved. Walking around with clouds over your head will only get you and your spouse so far. Being passive-aggressive with your behaviors and words will also only get you so far. Yes, conversations can be difficult to engage in, especially if you're the one in the wrong, or find it hard to admit when you're wrong, but you must have them to move forward. Marriage is not a destination. It's that dance that keeps going so long as you keep dancing. And when a challenging song comes on, or one of you trips up and falls to the floor, you should address it and work at it to keep moving forward.

Marriage can be tough.

* * * * *

You may need to compromise.

Our Story: We Win Some—We Lose Some.

Shared by Troy

We were excited to move to our seventh home. Unlike with previous homes, this was the first time we had to purchase a refrigerator, dishwasher, washing machine, etc. Of course, we were both super excited to find the best appliances that suited our style and the decor of our new home. I wanted all the appliances to be the same brand as the stove (already in the house), wanted the washer and dryer that had all the settings we'd never use, and wanted the refrigerator to be subzero. Shantel had her preferences, but just really wanted to stay within a certain budget and find the best within that. I agreed this made the most sense, and so we searched within our budget.

Finally, we got our selections down to a few options in each category. True to our nature, Shantel leaned more left, as I leaned more right. I had to remind her that in all the prior homes; I used these appliances more. Whether it be doing the dishes or washing the clothes, this was my forte. She looked at me with widening eyes. She agreed with what I was saying and knew I would be more inclined to keep up with those household duties if we purchased what excited me. So, she agreed to go with my selections. We both walked away, content with our choices. I got the appliances from the same brand. Shantel made sure we stayed within budget, and we both felt like we found the best in the parameters we set for ourselves.

Compromising has become second nature for us. We must compromise at least ten times a day. (And we wonder why Sage, our preschooler, is such a master negotiator.) Whether it be who's taking the kids to school; where we're going for our walk; what we're eating for lunch; what color decor we want; who's making dinner; where to order dinner from; who's walking Avery; who's putting which kid to bed; or what we're watching on TV… the compromises we make are endless.

> **DID YOU KNOW?**
> It's common for women to consider their husbands' opinions and feelings when making decisions. However, research indicates that men may not always reciprocate this behavior. Surprisingly, if straight men in relationships don't value their partner's input, there's a significant 81% chance of the marriage deteriorating. When couples, especially men, embrace and respect their partner's viewpoint, emotions, and needs in decision-making, they pave the way for mutually beneficial solutions, leading to positive outcomes for both (Benson 2023).

Our Thoughts

Like a business negotiation, in a partnership, no one walks away with everything they wanted, but hopefully they walk away content. You give a little; you get a little, and you hope you each get enough of what matters most so that you both walk away okay with the outcome. At times, one spouse may get what they want in one instance, knowing that the next time their partner will get what they want in the next. While some may love to compromise, others may hate it and need to work extra hard to overcome the feeling of not getting what they feel they deserve, need, or want.

For that reason, marriage can be tough.

* * * * *

You get stuck in your routines and find it difficult to balance your time.

Shantel's Story: The Workaholic

When I was working full time as an assistant principal, I worked long hours. I arrived at work by 7:30 a.m. on most days and usually got home around 5:00-5:30 p.m. (before Sage, it was even later). If it wasn't for Troy applying the pressure on me to come home each day, I probably would have been at work even longer. This was not because I loved my work that much, but it was because I got stuck in routines. I like to finish what I start, and yes... I am a workaholic. When I finally got home, I'd get a minute to change clothes, breathe, and then switch roles with Troy to get my time with Sage while also giving him a break. Our nighttime routine was just that, very routine. Every day looked pretty much the same because I was very strict when it came to Sage's bedtime (a lot changed with baby number two).

Because I was so routine oriented and always had "so much to do," it was real work to find time for me and Troy. It also took a lot of discipline to be present for others. When visiting family, I always brought my laptop, and when hanging out with friends, I'd work longer hours beforehand to make sure my work was complete. I missed out on great moments because of my inability to balance life, giving all the weight to work and my routine. I saw that if it wasn't planned for, most times it wouldn't happen. This wore on me. Thankfully, Troy was very vocal about his needs, and made sure I stepped up in being present, fully present—no laptops and no work in our marriage outside of "work time." Our marriage had to drive my routines; my routines could not drive our marriage.

> **Our marriage had to drive my routines; my routines could not drive our marriage.**

> **DID YOU KNOW?**
>
> "... couples in which one spouse is a workaholic are more likely to divorce than couples when neither party is a workaholic" (Robinson 2020).

Our Thoughts

As a married couple, you either have the entire day together (in some way shape, or form), or you have very limited time with each other, like we did. You may be always in each other's space and taking up each other's time (for the good/bad/indifferent), or you're planning how you spend your entire weekend/night with each other because you never get to spend time together during the week. You may be a homebody, while your spouse loves to be out. They may be a night owl, while you are a morning person. The thought of being with your spouse 24/7 can seem daunting or can feel like a dream come true.

Either way you slice it, regardless of if you're literally with each other all day, or no part of the day; if you live in the same house or sleep in different beds; share a meal or two together each day or only meet each other passing through the bathroom; the day-to-day routines can get old—fast. You know each other's smells, looks, behaviors, and sounds. You know when he's upset, or she's about to have her "time of the month." You know what the other person is going to say; how they feel; and even what day of the week they want to be left alone. The daily ins and outs of your schedules, if you're not careful, can force you both to lose the romance, spontaneity, and longing for each other you once had.

If you managed to find the *perfect* balance of time together and are **both** truly content with your marriage's ebb and flow... awesome!!! For many, though, this is still a work in progress, as life will continue to throw curve balls that force you together for time periods longer than you're used to (like the COVID-19 pandemic) or can force you apart (like a job relocation/promotion). Getting stuck in your routines or not having a balance of quality time with your spouse can lead to distraction or unnecessary conflict.

Marriage can be tough.

Closing Thoughts

Marriage can be tough for the reasons shared or the many topics not discussed, like limited control, inability to manage or talk about finances, the challenge of parenting, or having little in common once your children leave the home. While we know marriage can be the toughest partnership you will ever have, we also know how beautiful it can be when handled with care, effort, love, loyalty, and grace. To think that you possibly...

- were spread thin and came back from it,
- survived being with each other 24/7 throughout the pandemic/job loss,
- are mindful of your actions and how they impact your spouse,
- intentionally work to grow together, not apart,
- learned how to resolve conflict (or are getting better at it) and,
- compromise with each other time and time again.

You should give yourself and your marriage grace for all it has endured.

Through your marriage, no matter how long or short it's been, or *good* or *bad* it is, there are things you can intentionally do to strengthen it, nourish it, and elevate it. Many people recommend seeking counsel from pastoral ministries, therapists, or coaches, as well as taking vacations together, turning phones off at mealtime, or even taking solo getaways/retreats.

Becoming *Spartner*s (spouses who are business partners) is an alternate way to elevate and nourish your marriage. If you're winning in arguably the toughest partnership of all time—marriage—you can certainly win at a business partnership with your spouse. Not only can this generate more streams of income for your family, but it can also connect you and your spouse in ways only running a business can.

> **DID YOU KNOW?**
> "Adam and Eve 'complete' one another not by satisfying each other's personal desires, but by becoming unbreakable partners who seek the other's well-being" (Drimalla and BibleProject Team 2023).

Discover the Value in Your Spouse as a Business Partner...

Even though marriage is tough.

Marriage can be tough, but that doesn't mean it has to be tough for *you*. Try these strategies to help you discover the value in your spouse, and try to prevent or work through the tough parts of marriage that may come your way.

Strategies:

Prioritize Self-Care: Make a conscious effort to take time for self-care and ensure your cup is not empty. Schedule regular moments for yourself to recharge, whether it's a hobby, exercise, meditation, or simply downtime.

Communicate: Commit to open and honest communication with your spouse. Discuss your needs, wants, and expectations regularly. Do not let resentment build up; address issues as they arise.

Make Quality Time: Strive for a balance of quality time together and apart, understanding that too much or too little time together can lead to problems.

Embrace Change: Acknowledge that people change over time, and it's normal for interests and priorities to shift. Be open to embracing these changes together.

Give Grace and Appreciation: Show appreciation for each other's efforts in the marriage journey. Recognize the progress you've made and the hurdles you have overcome together.

Explore New Experiences: Consider trying new experiences together, like taking vacations or starting a business together. These can help you bond and create lasting memories as well as legacy.

* * * * *

Remember: Every marriage is unique and has been divinely put together to be great.

Reflect: Which strategies can you commit to trying in your marriage?

CHAPTER TWO
A Marriage and Business Partnership Can Thrive

―――⁂―――

*A business partnership with your spouse
can lead to a better marriage.*

Our Story: Going Nowhere Fast

Shared by Shantel

We were planning to have breakfast, go for a walk, and then shoot content. We were rushing, or so I thought. As I prepared breakfast, I saw Troy chilling on the couch, scrolling through his phone, and tossing a ball around with Phoenix. Soon, breakfast was ready, everyone ate, and I began to clean up. Troy continued to chill, play with Phoenix and then Avery. He appeared to be living his best life! I felt emotions creep up. I thought, *why was he just hanging out? Don't we need to go somewhere… and he rushes me?*

"Troy, can you get the boys ready?" I asked kindly, as I wrestled with the frustration and confusion of why he needed to be asked to do this.

"Yes, of course," he replied.

I cleaned the entire kitchen and vacuumed the floors. I went into the master closet to find Troy still ironing the boys' clothes. I asked, "What's taking so long?"

"I just needed to spread the bed, move *your* clothes out of the way, and take a breath *for me,*" Troy stated.

"Okay," I replied. I walked away, feeling even more frustrated.

Moments later, Troy approached me and told me he had been trying to get out of the house all morning. It was 10:30 a.m. then and way past the time he thought made sense to do all we planned to do.

"What you say and what you do… don't match. You said you wanted to get out of here this morning, but you're just taking your time," I said.

"You move slow all the time, but congratulations to *you* for being as productive as you were today. I came to the conclusion that we were not moving quickly this morning when we were still in the kids' room working, and it was 8:30," Troy proclaimed sarcastically.

"Well, next time, tell me when you decide to change your pace," I said. "I've been rushing."

"Well, it didn't look like it!" Troy snapped back.

From there, the conversation turned toward every direction an argument can go, further and further from the root problem, which was communication. One of us was ready to go for a walk alone with the kids, while the other was ready to go for a run alone and sweat out the frustration.

We had work to do, and content to shoot. We had goals for the day. These individual behaviors were not going to help us get our work done. Instead, they would draw us further from it. We both felt like we had to address the problem. We knew we had to problem solve. Certainly, we had to figure it out. Yes, we would eventually talk it out and resolve the issue as a married couple should, but by adding the layer of work-related goals, we felt more compelled to resolve this simple issue that had blown up (as many married-people arguments do).

So, in the heat of the argument, something magical happened. We stopped and stated what it was we needed from each other. I shared that I need Troy to communicate when he decides to rush or not, and Troy stated that he needs us to put time allotments on our plans/itineraries for each day.

Once we reached this understanding, we agreed that going our separate ways was *not* the best choice for our business or our marriage. By honing in on our communication, speaking to each other the way the other needed to be spoken to, expressing ourselves respectfully, and listening to what the other was really sharing, we were able to not only get the job done, but strengthen our marriage.

> *And above all things have fervent love for one another, for "love will cover a multitude of sins."*
>
> —1 PETER 4:8 NKJV

Our Thoughts

There is a plethora of ways your marriage and business can become better when you are both committed to both your marriage and business. The commitment to both is essential, but the commitment to the marital relationship is non-negotiable. If one person cares more about the business than their marital relationship, the relationship can feel transactional and distant. Over time, the relationship can feel more like a typical business relationship but become more problematic as deep emotions are involved. If one spouse cares more for the marriage, then at worst, the productivity of the business may slow down, but the marriage will get better.

Knowing what you need to do in your marriage is one thing, but actually doing it for the betterment of your marriage (and ultimately your business) is another.

Knowing what you need to do in your marriage is one thing, but actually doing it for the betterment of your marriage (and ultimately your business) is another. Thus, both marriage and business will increase.

A business partnership with your spouse can lead to **Better Communication**.

* * * * *

> *"Love is not only something you feel, it is something you do."*
>
> —DAVID WILKERSON

Our Story: We still argue... just better!

Shared by Shantel.

Being in business together has definitely enhanced our level of communication. We've always had respect for each other, but we haven't always expressed it the best during moments of frustration. In the past, Troy would do something to upset me, and I would never address it in real-time. Troy would have no idea that I was upset until I blindsided him days, weeks, or even months later. Troy did not like my passive-aggressive approach and definitely knew it was not the way to communicate with him. In return, I did not like how Troy would deflect in the middle of arguments, as it almost always brought us off track from what we were actually arguing about.

This changed (well, got a lot better) when we started working together. There was immediately an added layer of care and intention in our verbal disputes. We no longer had time to give in to our egos or harbor over minor things. If we continued to press on the way we did prior, it would impact both our marriage as well as our business, and we had goals in both areas. We worked together to get to the root cause of our problems, and we let things go faster so we could move forward, instead of: raising our voices over each other; not listening with intent or taking accountability; being passive-aggressive; deflecting; resisting apologizing so we could prove our individual points; or asking the ever-so-classic phrase, "Are you done?" (basically initiating World War III).

Since working together, we have moved from arguing to having disagreements with the intent of truly listening and understanding how the other person feels. Of course, we still have tiffs, we can bump heads, and some arguments don't go that smoothly. However, these arguments do not get nearly as heightened nor do the "blow overs" last nearly as long as before. The frequency of these disputes is far less than before. Without a doubt, becoming *Spartners* has positively impacted our communication in our marriage.

> *Understand this, my dear brothers and sisters:*
> *You must all be quick to listen, slow to speak, and slow to get angry.*
>
> —JAMES 1:19 NLT

Our Thoughts

Learning to communicate better as *Spartners* has a direct carryover into your marriage. When both partners feel seen and heard, it allows for a stronger and deeper connection to be shared. Not only will this have a positive impact on the trajectory of your business, but it also enriches your marriage in ways you did not know were possible. When communication is a priority in your *Spartner*ship, you are more invested and committed to each other and your work, thus both your marriage and business reap the benefits.

A business partnership with your spouse can lead to **Stronger Intimacy**.

> *Always be humble and gentle. Be patient with each other, making allowance for each other's faults because of your love. Make every effort to keep yourselves united in the Spirit, binding yourselves together with peace.*
>
> —EPHESIANS 4:2-3 NLT

Our Story: My Work Wife is My Real Wife

Shared by Troy.

We've always had a romantic, passionate relationship. Back in the early days, before kids, we'd be up in the wee hours of the morning showing our love for one another. We'd be up late at night, with candles lit, hand in hand, snuggled and cuddled up. We ensured we made each other feel loved and desired. After kids, the intentions were there, of course, but so were the three-times-a-night wakeups, tossing and turning at night, late hours in the office, and everything else that follows having kids with full-time, stressful careers. We never strayed away, but we definitely were not as close or connected as we had been. We didn't have as much quality time with one another, no matter how hard we tried. Between checking to see how social media posts were performing, writing teacher evaluations, and taking care of a child, there was little time for romance, deep conversation, and daily connection.

Once we began working together, however, our intimacy hit new levels. We show more passion for each other, not only physically, but spiritually. We have more respect and appreciation for each other's life experiences and past careers, as we see certain skills we picked up along the way benefiting our business today. We feel reignited and reborn in our sexual life, as we touch more, pray more, and show up for each other more when needed.

We connect more through shared experiences and conversations. For example, our conversations are no longer surface-based like, "How was your day?" or "Whatever happened with..." or "What did you do today?" Instead, it's much deeper. Conversations now start with, "I'm not sure how we should..." and "I really loved when..." or "How did you feel when we...?"

Finally, we have more quality time. Quality time to refuel our passion, define our purpose, and enhance our love for each other. Working together has truly given us a greater level of appreciation for the time we spend together.

We never realized how much our intimacy could skyrocket by working with each other. As the endorphins rush when a large deal is made, a project is complete, or a new opportunity comes, we have each other to embrace, celebrate with, and appreciate. I officially get to say, "My *work* wife is my *real* wife." We now have each other, and it feels so good on every level!

> *Then the LORD God said, "It is not good that the man should be alone; I will make him a helper fit for him."*
>
> —GENESIS 2:18 ESV

Our Thoughts

Building a *Spartner*ship can do wonders for your intimacy. You will connect in a deeper and more meaningful way. Seeing each other work toward a common goal will enhance your level of appreciation and attraction for one another. Participating in thought-provoking and meaningful conversations will arouse you in ways potentially unfelt before, connecting you at deeper levels. These are major components of intimacy. When you work with your spouse, and you both truly give it your best, you will value your spouse more, leading to heightened love, passion, and intimacy, thus reigniting the passion and fire your marriage deserves.

A business partnership with your spouse can lead to **Deeper Connection**.

> *Therefore comfort each other and edify one another, just as you also are doing.*
>
> —1 THESSALONIANS 5:11 NKJV

Troy's Story: You Can't Connect Without *The Connector*

It was nearing the close of a very productive workday; we still had to go over a few things including content strategy, shoot location, and content pitches for brands. We were both exhausted, and it felt like we were working nonstop. In these moments, agitation, tiredness, and the need for decompression are at a high.

Normally when I am tired or *over* something, I can be a bit short. I may sharply say, "Okay, let's wrap this up," or even be dismissive of the ideas or thoughts of others. This approach never works for Shantel and usually sets us back from getting our work done more times than not. It can also agitate her and cause her to pull back and disconnect from me.

This day was different, though. Instead of being short, I asked Shantel for a quick second to pray over us and our work. This reset and refocused me, as well as creating space for the Spirit to take charge. Instead of Shantel withdrawing herself from me, she connected more deeply with me.

In our marriage, Jesus remains at the center and is who we call upon daily to deepen our connection. When we began to call on Him in our business, the connection grew more intense as we saw how He can show up in *all* forms, at *all* times, in *all* ways. Now, we have had more opportunities to connect with each other, thus making our relationship deeper, more meaningful and fruitful.

Our Thoughts

When you are married, of course, your connection with each other should grow deeper. There are ups and downs, good times, and challenging times. Those experiences should help strengthen your marriage. While the great times of traveling, buying a new house, or having a baby, for example, may draw you closer to each other, so can hitting a low point, as you can be drawn into each other for support, compassion, and love.

If you work in a field where you do not have many people to talk to about the work you do, it's easy to feel alone and disconnected. There's a smaller (if any) network of like-minded people who you can connect with, thus making the work potentially all the more stressful or *un*enjoyable. When you work with your spouse, however, you now have someone who understands what you go through, day to day, firsthand.

Live your life of marriage and business in the "**HOV**" lane. Focus on being **H**onest, **O**pen and **V**ulnerable. Being honest with each other adds a new layer of openness in your marriage. It makes it easier to be vulnerable, thus deepening your connection.

A business partnership with your spouse can lead to **More Quality Time**.

Shantel's Story: No Longer Living for the Weekends

As I scroll through my Instagram posts over the last few years, I notice one major thing (besides a growing family, new scenery, and me and Troy aging like fine wine). I see that the moments I posted most happened on the weekends.

Here are some posts "pre-*Spartners*"

March 17, 2019
Sunday Famday 🖤

November 5, 2019
Woodsy weekends 🖤. Beyond grateful for the light that shows beauty, the air that brings peace, and the waves that bring joy. We are so blessed and grateful. Weekend vibes, daily thanks!

September 27, 2020
What a great Sunday!! Here's just a teaser! Pumpkin extravaganza! @troy_brooks

November 14, 2020
Just another Saturday ...

Here are some posts from once we became *Spartners*.

April 13, 2022
Working alongside @troy_brooks has opened me up to a world I really never considered for me- the #entrepreneurlife world. It's been such a blessing to raise our family together and spend quality time with each other every day.

To make this choice wasn't easy or fast. There was definitely a rub of *Do I leave my career to help his career takeoff, OR do I focus on building my own empire?* The honest truth is ... there is no *his* or *mine* in our partnership. From friendship to marriage, to our professional partnership, we are a TEAM with one shared vision: raise our kids on OUR TIME with the FREEDOM we set for ourselves.

Working with your spouse ain't for everyone, but it's definitely for us!

Cheers to the power couples creating their lives together, literally brick by brick.

June 16, 2022

I am grateful for starting and ending my days with this crew, //teambrooks.

We take Sage to school as a family most days, spend quality time together while he learns with his friends at school, and then pick him up and partake in more family quality time. Every day isn't as fun as this one was, but they sure are as loving and amazing.

Feeling gratitude daily.

July 10, 2022

Wow, what an awesome family vacation?!!! I feel so blessed and so grateful to have spent this last week doing the things we love with the people we love!

This vacay was epic!!! Staying outside, laughing, loving and doing it all together is what made this so great! The drinks, great food and awesome vibes also helped too!! 🤪.

Happy Summer y'all

A MARRIAGE AND BUSINESS PARTNERSHIP CAN THRIVE

July 28, 2022

Just another day in July............Usually, around this time each year, I'd just be finishing up my summer work for my school and getting ready to take off a month from the forever-so-stressful education system.

I'll be exhausted, eager, and beyond ready to spend extra time with my family and friends. I have an ever-so-packed schedule of all the things to do and see, trying to squeeze in every bit of summer vacation I could.

But this July is different; I mean way different.

I'm not stressed; I'm not exhausted, and I have all the time I want and need to spend with my family and friends. I am free. I have the autonomy I've been longing for.

I'm doing great work with my biz partner @troy_brooks, and I feel validated.

Most importantly, I'm filled with joy doing the things we love... while getting paid for it!

Today is just another day in July.
But one I would never trade in and always remember.

What difference do you see? Besides the amount of time I have to actually write and share my thoughts and feelings (as evidenced by the number of words), I am also so alive in the messaging because of the time I have to invest in myself and my family. These moments are filled with an abundance of quality. Quality time I will never take for granted.

> **DID YOU KNOW?**
>
> When people are socially connected and have stable and supportive relationships, they are more likely to make healthy choices and have better mental and physical health outcomes. They are also better able to cope with hard times, stress, anxiety, and depression (Centers for Disease Control and Prevention 2023).

Our Story: Beyond Summer

Shared by Troy

Working together full time has truly been a blessing. We know what life looked like before this, and wow, what a difference! In Shantel's Instagram caption, "Just another day in July," she expressed the pressure she would normally be under in the month of July. She would just be finishing up a heavy summer workload and be prepared to enjoy one month without work by cramming in everything she could. This was her life for nine of the fifteen years she was in education.

That was also our life together, always having to plan trips and outings around her summer vacation or spring breaks because scheduling work outside these timelines was not allowed. Though we recognized the blessing of still having this time, it was also the worst times to travel and the most expensive. It didn't give us much freedom or mobility to enjoy summer much together, or just each other, for that matter. The amount of quality time we have working together full time has allowed us to foster our marriage and be present for our children. We love summer, but now we also get to enjoy summer, fall, winter, and spring.

> **We love summer, but now we also get to enjoy summer, fall, winter, and spring.**

Growing our business together still feels surreal at times. Gone are the days of me bringing Shantel food to work, giving her a hug, and driving off because she could not leave the building for a real lunch date. We now have lunch dates and work dates! Since *Spartner*ing, we have the freedom we desire and the ability to be the people we want to be—intentional, strong, connected, loving, present, caring and involved spouses and parents who can give their children the time and experiences they deserve. We can be strong and successful business partners who do impactful work while leaving a legacy of our own.

* * * * *

A Spartners' Story:

Julien and Kiersten Saunders (*rich & REGULAR*)

*Spartner*s Julien and Kiersten Saunders are founders of rich & REGULAR, a media production business, and have been married since 2015. Since 2017, they've worked together as full-time authors, speakers, and creators under rich & REGULAR. Prior to this, however, they were coworkers, so they've actually worked together since they met in 2012.

They, too, have witnessed their marriage strengthen by working together in their own business. They share that, "It's a privilege to watch your partner grow before your very eyes. As parents, we naturally marvel at our children's growth and can see when they've mastered a skill or overcome a fear over a period of time. But as *Spartners*, you have the same experience." They go on to share the inspiration they receive by having a front-row seat in seeing each other go from being uncomfortable with something new to mastering that skill or conquering that fear. For the Saunders, when they are faced with new fears or discomforts, they can remind each other of the last time they felt that way and motivate each other to rise above it, thus deepening their levels of connection.

SPARTNERS

* * * * *

A Spartners' Story:

Justin and April Moore (*social media creators*)

*Spartner*s Justin and April Moore have been married since 2011. They have worked together since 2009 and run a social media creator's business. They have found much value within their marriage by working together. They share that their communication experienced massive improvement. "Since our life IS our work, any issues that come up in our personal lives AND business require us to address them with objectivity, love, and understanding," they explain. Like us, they were forced to learn how to communicate better if they wanted their business to thrive. With more time in the day to practice, it is only natural for it to get better, as it has for us all!

* * * * *

A Spartners' Story:

Justin and Laura Lagrotta (*Metro Tours*)

For *Spartners* Justin and Laura, married since 2017, and cofounders of Metro Tours (a tour guide business serving New York City since 2019), sharing in their successes together gave them a deeper connection and appreciation for each other. Laura shares that although they were already doing their individual jobs, side by side, and saw parts of each other they normally would never see, Justin's passion for Metro Tours was heartwarming, and deepened their connection even more. Justin shared similar sentiments and found joy in building something out of nothing. "We accomplished something, and it felt like our marriage was better," he shares.

* * * * *

A Spartners' Story:

Wes and Veronica Güity (*Grace and Lamb*)

Last, for *Spartners* Wes and Veronica Güity, married since 2013 and *officially* working together since 2021, Grace & Lamb, "*Spartner*ing up" has brought a mirror into their marriage where they get to really look at themselves, engage in open dialogue, set the right expectations, and work within each other's bandwidth, not just professionally, but personally. They have discussions that lay out their roles of who does what and what percentage of the load they will hold, whether that be in parenting or running their business. For example, Veronica shares that when she was in her third trimester of pregnancy, "I felt guilty not being able to do as much as I wanted." She was exhausted.

Through open dialogue, reviewing their bandwidth, and setting realistic expectations, Wes was able to reassure her that this was what being a *Spartner* was all about. He told her, "You will have your time." In that moment, though, it was *his* time to hold it down, as he did, connecting them at deeper levels.

> *Love is patient, love is kind. It does not envy, it does not boast, it is not proud. It does not dishonor others, it is not self-seeking, it is not easily angered, it keeps no record of wrongs. Love does not delight in evil but rejoices with the truth. It always protects, always trusts, always hopes, always perseveres.*
>
> —1 CORINTHIANS 13:4-7 NIV

Our Thoughts

A *Spartner*ship can lead to a better marriage by enhancing many key foundational elements. It can **improve your communication skills**, allowing for productive conversation around disagreements, constructive feedback, and more meaningful conversations. It can **strengthen your levels of intimacy**, allowing you to be more vulnerable and honest with each other, thus unmasking the layers of protection you carry each day. A *Spartner*ship can **deepen your connection,** reigniting the sparks that helped you fall in love with your spouse to begin with, as well as create new sparks, as you now see them in new ways. It can provide you with **more quality time**, allowing you to share moments with each other and those you love more often and with more intention and presence.

We encourage you to live your life of marriage and business in the **HOV** lane. Focus on being **H**onest, **O**pen and **V**ulnerable. Being honest with each other adds a new layer of openness in your marriage. It makes it easier to be vulnerable, thus deepening your connection.

All marriages take work, just like all business and work relationships. There will certainly be conflict, stress, tears, and moments of feeling defeated. It is critical that, just like in marriage, you work together to rise above it. The work you put in at the beginning of your *Spartner*ship will determine the success you reap later, in one way, shape, or form.

To get there, you must be willing to get on the same page and the same beat... as you dance to the same song.

> *A person standing alone can be attacked and defeated, but two can stand back-to-back and conquer. Three are even better, for a triple-braided cord is not easily broken.*
>
> —ECCLESIASTES 4:12 NLT

Discover the Value in Your Spouse as a Business Partner...

It can elevate your marriage.

Enriching your marriage is a "get to" not a "have to." Read the **Get to** topics below and take time to reflect on what each looks like in your marriage.

Get to: Enhanced Communication

Working together as *Spartners* necessitates effective communication. When both partners feel heard and understood in a professional setting, these communication skills naturally carry over into your marriage, resulting in improved dialogue and connection.

> *Reflect:* How does effective communication as *Spartners* translate into deeper dialogue and connection within your marriage?

Get to: Deeper Intimacy

The shared commitment and collaboration of a business partnership can lead to a deeper and more meaningful connection between spouses. Witnessing each other's dedication and effort can increase mutual appreciation and attraction, ultimately enhancing intimacy in your marriage.

> *Reflect:* In what ways does witnessing your partner's dedication and effort in business deepen your appreciation and attraction in your marriage?

Get to: Shared Goals

In a *Spartner*ship, you work toward common goals and objectives. This shared sense of purpose can strengthen your bond, as you both have a vested interest in the success of your business. Transferring this shared commitment to your marriage can lead to a stronger partnership in all aspects of life.

Reflect: How can shared business goals strengthen your bond, and how can this commitment transfer to enrich your marriage?

Get to: Increased Support

When you work closely with your spouse, you gain a unique support system. You understand each other's professional challenges and can offer emotional support and guidance. This added layer of trust and support can deepen your connection in your marriage as well.

Reflect: How does understanding each other's professional challenges enhance the support and trust within your marriage?

Get to: More Quality Time

A *Spartner*ship involves spending more time together. This can lead to more intentional and meaningful moments shared both at work and in your personal life. The increased quality time can help you connect on a deeper level in your marriage.

Reflect: How does increased time together in both work and personal life foster deeper connections and more meaningful moments in your marriage?

Get to: Better Conflict Resolution

Handling disagreements and conflicts as business partners can improve your conflict resolution skills in your marriage. You become more adept at addressing issues constructively and finding mutually beneficial solutions.

Reflect: In what ways does handling conflicts constructively as business partners improve conflict resolution skills and understanding in your marriage?

Get to: Alignment of Values

A successful business partnership requires alignment of values and goals. This alignment can spill over into your personal life, ensuring that you and your spouse are on the same page as it relates to your shared values, aspirations, and priorities.

Reflect: How does aligning values and goals in business spill over into your personal life, shaping shared values and priorities in your marriage?

Get to: Increased Trust

Trust is a cornerstone of any successful business partnership. When you trust your spouse as a business partner, it reinforces the trust you have in your marriage. This trust can lead to a stronger sense of security and connection.

Reflect: How does trusting your spouse as a business partner reinforce and deepen the trust within your marriage?

Get to: Shared Passion

Sharing a professional passion and working toward common business goals can reignite the passion in your marriage. The excitement and enthusiasm you have for your work can spill over into your personal life.

Reflect: How does sharing a professional passion and pursuing common goals reignite the passion and enthusiasm within your marriage?

CHAPTER THREE
Guess What? You Married on Purpose!

What's your love story?

Shantel's Story: Our Love Story

Troy and I had been friends since our middle school years. I was 12; he was 13. We were just friends. Of all the negative memories I had of my two years in junior high school, there were very few positive ones. Troy was a positive memory for me, which is a big deal if you knew my middle school stories!

Years passed by and we would see each other here and there, depending on where the wind blew. Once we crossed paths in a bagel shop in Queens. I was with my boyfriend at the time, and he was with his then fiancé. We said, "Hi," smiled, and kept it moving. We were always platonic, always friendly, and always had nothing but love for each other.

A few more years passed, and we connected again on the infamous Facebook. Troy was party promoting, and I was a party girl. He invited me out to join him a few times, and I dismissed it each time. Not for any specific reason, but I had other plans. One day, he ran into one of our mutual friends in Los Angeles while he was living there. They both messaged me and said how crazy it was to run into each other. The next day, I went to Facebook, clicked into the search toolbar, and typed "Troy Brooks." *What was he up to these days, anyway?* I wondered.

He had a great profile picture of himself. He was strong, attractive, and just radiated something different that I hadn't noticed before. So, like any Facebook stalker, I began to scroll. I didn't see a photo of him with his fiancé anywhere. *Were they still together?* "Let me scroll some more," I said to myself. "Hmm... nothing." I scrolled some more. Still nothing. While scrolling, however, I *did* see that he loved great food, enjoyed traveling, served at his church, and just seemed fun. I also saw he had moved back to New York and just started his own fitness business out of New York City.

Hmm... I work out... I've had my fair share of trainers... I don't really need a trainer, but I do have this wedding coming up in a few months, I thought to myself. *Yeah, I know I live like an hour away, but... why not?* I reassured myself.

So, I messaged him. I used a different tone, the "xo" signature, and was definitely more assertive than any prior message. He had no clue what I was up to but was about his work. See the message below.

I remember meeting him for the first time in years. It was so weird; it just felt so different from any other time I saw *him*, or any old friend, for that matter. He greeted me with that same love and chill we always had. He was excited to see that he was now taller than me.

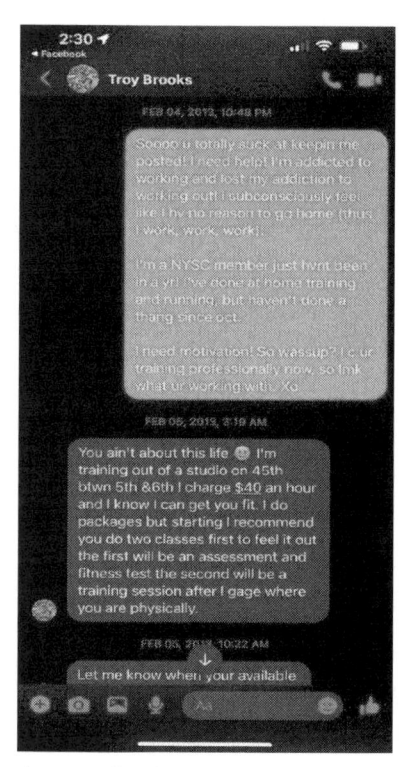

(My Facebook message to Troy initiating our relationship.

My conversation is on the right, Troy's is on the left.)

SPARTNERS

*This is us in junior high school in 1997.
I'm taller!*

This is us, newly engaged in December 2013. Yeah, he grew!

He showed me the studio where he worked. We chatted it up a bit; he gave me a killer workout; and we agreed to train twice a week, every Monday and Thursday. The next session we planned ironically fell on February 14, 2013—a Thursday and Valentine's Day. I quickly told him we didn't have to meet if he already had plans. He told me he didn't and would love to train me. So, like any two young New Yorkers, we agreed to train and then go out for drinks. No, this was not his M.O. if that's what you're thinking. I, too, made *him* feel different. There was something definitely unique about what we were building.

That Thursday came quickly. We trained once more and then got drinks across the street at a very intimate Italian restaurant. Before he could take a sip of his drink, I began to quiz him, asking him all the questions you're not supposed to ask on a first date (so they say).

"Do you want kids? How many?"

"Where do you see yourself in five years?"

"What gets you excited?"

"What is one challenge you've overcome?"

"How's your relationship with your mom?"

I asked it *all*. Troy couldn't believe all the questions that were coming out of my mouth. I think he was actually frozen in disbelief like, "What did I just walk into?" I then told him that if we were going to actually date (I knew what I wanted and found no reason to beat around the bush), I'd need him to take the Strengths Finder 2.0 test. (If you don't know about this test, check it out)! This test is used for business, but I wanted to use it for our relationship. Why would I want to know what strengths, assets, and perspective my colleagues have at work, but not my guy at home? To me, this always went hand in hand. Who knew how this would show back up in our lives almost 10 years later! God works!

So, after picking up his mouth from the floor, he said, "Sure, I'll take it."

We proceeded to drink, eat, and converse some more. For the record, I was never *that* girl—the one who was assertive, demanding, and empowered to be herself, with no filter in an intimate relationship. For some reason, though, it was with Troy that I felt I could be ME. I could just cut to the chase and be ME. And he loved it... clearly.

Now faith is confidence in what we hope for and assurance about what we do not see.

—HEBREWS 11:1 NIV

Our Thoughts

Everyone has their own love story. We share ours because it always gives us those *feels* of excitement and wonder, as well as that spirit that brought us together so intensely, AND because remembering why you fell in love can potentially reinvigorate your marriage. Knowing your *why* is essential to anything we do in life, and remembering why you were attracted to this person might be the reset you need for your marriage and the spark for an amazing business partnership—a *Spartner*ship.

> **Knowing your *why* is essential to anything we do in life, and remembering why you were attracted to this person might be the reset you need for your marriage and the spark for an amazing business partnership—a *Spartner*ship.**

There was a fire, a longing, and a desire to have your partner in the beginning. Perhaps you were the person who was always "hard to get" and this time *you* had to do the chasing (like Shantel). Or perhaps you were good friends for years and then one day something just changed (like us). Or perhaps you literally just caught eyes from across the café and it was a done deal before it even started. Whatever your story, reflect on it. Relive it. Re-experience it for all the joy, stress, excitement, and the love. Tapping back into those *feels* can help you feel gratitude and assurance for why you are together today.

If you have been working on your marriage, you hopefully have a longing for your partner that supersedes what you had in the beginning. If you have allowed your marriage simply to *happen* as a result of saying, "I do," reflecting on your *why* can help you recalibrate and recenter on the core values you shared in the beginning, and the core values you share today.

> **DID YOU KNOW?**
>
> In an interview with married couple Richard Schwartz and Jacqueline Olds, both associate professors of psychiatry at Harvard Medical School and consultants to McLean and Massachusetts General hospitals, Olds said:
>
> "You have a tidal-like motion of closeness and drifting apart, closeness and drifting apart... And you have to have one person have a 'distance alarm' to notice the drifting apart so there can be a reconnection ... One could say that in the couples who are most successful at keeping their relationship alive over the years, there's an element of companionate love and an element of passionate love. And those each get reawakened in that drifting back and forth, the ebb and flow of lasting relationships" (Powell 2018).

The person you trust most is your spouse.

Troy's Story: Never Put All Your Eggs Into One Basket

My fitness career was booming. It was 2017, and I was now working for one of the hottest small group fitness gyms in New York City. I continued to take personal clients, but it was where I was a small group fitness coach that my name really began to circulate throughout the city and beyond. Shantel had just started a new position, too, as an assistant principal about 60-75 minutes from our home. This was a major win, not just because of the impact she would leave, but also because it provided her with the highest paid salary she'd ever had—about twice what she had previously been making. Together, we were a power couple in our industries, making an impact and making great income.

It wasn't before long, however, that her commute began to wear on her. It took about 60 minutes for her to get to work in the morning (leaving before 6:00 a.m.), and 90 minutes to sometimes two hours getting home because of traffic. We were also about 18 months into trying to conceive our first child, which was causing a lot of stress as well. We hoped to tough it out for a year, so we could save all the money we were making, but I saw the wear and tear it was causing on her body and spirit. She barely had the energy to enjoy the fruits of our labor or try at conceiving a baby. Shantel was exhausted.

So, we made the choice to move to the suburbs, closer to her new job. The place we found was amazing. It was a condo in White Plains, New York, right off a bustling strip of restaurants and shops. Plus, it was within walking distance of Whole Foods and only 20-30 minutes from everywhere we wanted to go. It was great! It was also three times the amount of rent as our coop mortgage and came with new bills. Still, we knew we were making a great income together and it would enhance our lifestyle and give her back so much time, energy, and life—it was a priceless decision. We signed our contract to move on November 1, 2017.

Days after signing our lease, I was pulled into an impromptu meeting with the owner of the boutique gym where I trained. She had her "second in command" and the head trainer present. *What is happening?* I wondered, as I cautiously walked to the table. After a long discussion, it turned out, I wasn't a "good fit." I was given a small severance, and we parted ways. I was laid off days after.

We were depending on my income to help pay for all the new expenses we had just signed up for. I was mortified. I knew to never put all my eggs into one basket, and although I still had some personal clientele, my main focus and priority was this gym. Regrettably, I had done what I swore not to do: I worked for someone else, gave them power over my livelihood, and it was taken away... just like that... just like I knew it could be.

I felt devalued and defeated, but worse, I felt I had let Shantel down. Thankfully, I also knew that Shantel would have my back. I trusted her. I trusted she would support me and work with me to figure out our next steps, not tear me down. I trusted she would listen to me and trust me, not judge me or doubt me. Losing this job was one of the hardest hits to me for a few reasons, and it could have been so much worse if I had not had a partner whom I trusted to be vulnerable and honest with.

> *When you go through deep waters, I will be with you. When you go through rivers of difficulty, you will not drown. When you walk through the fire of oppression, you will not be burned up; the flames will not consume you.*
>
> ISAIAH 43:2 NLT

Our Thoughts

You married your spouse and took the vows: "...to keep him/her for better or worse, for richer or poorer, in sickness and in health, and forsaking all others; be faithful only to him/her, so long as you both shall live."

These words reflect the sacred covenant of marriage. (*See* Genesis 2:20-25.)

There is no one physically on this planet you should trust more than your spouse. Therefore, it shouldn't be too far-fetched to trust your spouse when pitching to companies, attending important meetings, signing contracts, negotiating deals, scouting venues for events, or making grand decisions that will impact the direction of your business. In a healthy marriage, you trust your spouse, and your spouse trusts you. Your spouse is ultimately the best person to have by your side (potentially) in both marriage and business.

Going into business with someone you doubt, question, or feel slightly skeptic about can be a recipe for disaster. If you have to think about their agenda, question their morals or integrity, or whether finances would be difficult to discuss, it can be a burden on your business. Furthermore, these thoughts take away precious energy and time that could be devoted to growing your business.

We all want our businesses to thrive, and trust is a major pillar in the foundation of your business. When you have a *Spartner*, you can trust them. Your *Spartner* has your best interest at heart, and the best part is, they can now win *with* you, side by side.

* * * * *

Your partner is a boss!

Shantel's Story: He Made a Choice. Impact > Income

I was always in awe of Troy and his hunger to do more and be more. He is a natural-born hustler. When we first reconnected, he was a party promoter. I always thought it was for the look, the glam, and the fun, but for him, it was a surefire way to make great money quickly. Yes, the hours were tough, but he was great at what he did and found ways to build community, have fun, and make money from it. It was then that I really began to explore what I was doing with myself. I loved what I did to an extent, but it didn't look the same way on me as it did on him.

Troy had just started his own fitness business, stepping out all the way on his own as he knew his worth and he knew his needs. He knew he could not work for someone. He had to be his own boss. I loved that about him as well. Regardless of what was thrown his way, he was going to be his own boss and build his own empire. When we got married, he saw that party promoting wasn't going to allow for the lifestyle we wanted as a married couple. Yes, it was great money, but it was not a career for him or the legacy he wanted to build for us. I admired how he walked out of his last gig and fully into his fitness career. It took more hours to get the same income, but he was ready to put in the work and invest in himself and others because it felt right.

This was a major success for me. This is where I learned from him that every dollar isn't a good dollar. He could no longer fill you with drinks at night, and then provide motivational speaking and weights in the morning. He had to make a choice, and I loved the choice he made. This was the first of many successes he's made during our time together, and it's the one I share here because it's why I stay in love with him so hard and know we will always be okay. He will always make the necessary choices for us as a union, no matter what. Because I know this, I know he will always be the best father for our children, husband to me, and *Spartner* for our life together.

> *Wives, submit yourselves to your own husbands as you do to the Lord. For the husband is the head of the wife as Christ is the head of the church, his body, of which he is the Savior. Now as the church submits to Christ, so also wives should submit to their husbands in everything.*
>
> —EPHESIANS 5:22-24 NIV

Troy's Story: She Used Her Gifts for Us

Shantel embodies the definition of effective leadership. When I reconnected with her later in life, she was highly focused on enhancing the experiences of the children at the school she founded in Bedford-Stuyvesant, Brooklyn. She loved kids; it indeed showed, and the kids loved her back. She would often get letters from them, and some even asked to eat lunch in her office or help out before or after school.

Shantel has a way of making people feel seen, comfortable, and safe in her presence. I remember her telling me that it was pivotal to be present in kids' lives at that age because they are impressionable, and she can positively impact where they go in the future. She took her role of power and influence seriously. Shantel truly cared. She knew her goal was to be impactful in the lives of many, and she intentionally worked toward that daily.

Shantel knew she was supposed to plant seeds in that location to help the community flourish. She set a goal of five years at this school, but God had other plans. After two years, she took a different leader-building position in a new school district. During this season, I witnessed her impact policy as well as teaching and learning. She worked on strengthening social and emotional learning and was able to speak at NYU and share her message. She was also awarded a grant to attend Yale for a program partnership and was named Woman of Distinction in the community she served. Seeing Shantel work, empower and nurture others helped me see her as the naturally gifted and powerful leader she is today.

I knew she was great in all the spaces to which she devoted time. I valued her work ethic and commitment. There was no question in my mind that she would bring any less energy to the work we do together.

> *Houses and riches are an inheritance from fathers,*
> *But a prudent wife is from the LORD.*
>
> PROVERBS 19:14 NKJV

Our Thoughts

When considering working with your spouse as your business partner, it is important to reflect on the professional successes they've already had, as it can add more value to your *Spartner*ship.

What is it about them, professionally, that gave you the green light to get married? Do they have a strong work ethic? Are they committed to serving? Do they treat their colleagues like family? Do they speak on panels eloquently? Can they fix a problem with a car as if they can see right through it? Do they step into a classroom and command it? Have they been nominated for an award, saved someone's life, or won a case? No matter the success, there is something about who they were to achieve success that is important to explore, as it is a characteristic that can be vital to the success of your *Spartner*ship.

In one way, shape, or form, your spouse has been successful, which means what you do together can be successful. You may ask, "What if they've had *no* success?" One, we challenge you to reflect on how you both measure or identify *success*. Two, we ask that you weigh that information into whether you think your spouse can be successful working with you.

> **DID YOU KNOW?**
>
> Based on a Carnegie Mellon study, couples who are encouraging and supportive to each other experience more personal growth, happiness, psychological well-being, and better relationships (Zetlin 2020).

* * * * *

You are the Yin to Their Yang

Our Story: The Extrovert and the Introvert

Shared by Troy

We know each other's strengths and shortcomings better than anyone. We use these strengths and areas of growth to our advantage in both our marriage and business. For example, Shantel is more introverted. While she enjoys big events and parties, at times she can feel socially overwhelmed and thus finds it difficult to socialize organically. One of the qualities that attracted Shantel to me, interestingly, was *my* big, outgoing, extroverted personality.

In our marriage, we are able to leverage this dynamic in ways that allow us both to feel loved and accepted. At work, the same is true. At big events/parties, I can "work the room," network, and build contacts, while Shantel engages in a way she feels best, without the expectation of performing. We trust each other to work within our strengths. I connect with multiple people with my giving spirit and gravitational energy.

Shantel adds her layer of sincerity, peace, and structure, which balances us out.

> **DID YOU KNOW?**
> "Creating shared meaning is one of the most rewarding facets of a marriage. It can be awesome, messy, agonizing, joyous, elusive, fun, risky, maddening, invigorating, mysterious, and all of these at once. If you start your relationship off by ensuring that it's meaningful, you can save yourself a lot of pain and heartache down the road" (Brittle 2020).

Closing Thoughts

Successful spouses move in unison with the same visions, goals, and desired outcomes. The same principles apply in business. You want to know that you and your business partner are aligned and that you have the same vision and goals for your business. Knowing each other's strengths and areas of opportunity allows you to be most effective.

There's no better partner for you than the one you married.

If you are in a healthy marriage, then you most likely married your spouse because:

- You have a special love story.
- You can trust them.
- They support you.
- You are the yin to their yang.
- They make you feel seen, heard, and respected.
- They believe in you.

What would you want from a business partner that you haven't already harvested with your spouse? Your spouse knows your dance moves, your spirit, and your ways. You choose your dance partner, your spouse, for a reason, right? They are the best partner for you, not just in marriage where you trust them, balance them, and love them; and not just in parenting, where you depend on them and grow with them. They are the best partner for you when hanging out, where you share your interests and friends; but also in life, where you work together to reach common goals and stand on the same foundation.

So, can they also be your best partner in business, where you prioritize your professional goals, work in your strengths, and build your legacy together?

> *And he said, "'This explains why a man leaves his father and mother and is joined to his wife, and the two are united into one.' Since they are no longer two but one, let no one split apart what God has joined together."*
>
> —MATTHEW 19:5-6 NLT

Discover the Value in Your Spouse as a Business Partner...

They were the right one *then*, they are the best one *now*.

Try these strategies to help you discover the value in your spouse:

1. Reflect on Your Love Story:

- Carve out 30 minutes to reminisce about how you met and fell in love.

    Reflect: How can you use this shared history as a source of motivation and inspiration for your business partnership?

2. Identify Your Why:

- Create a list of reasons why you were initially attracted to each other and why you chose to marry each other. Share your list with each other.

    (Knowing your *why* can help you recenter on your core values, both in your marriage and in your business endeavors.)

    Reflect: How can reflecting on your reasons for why you chose to marry each other help you appreciate each other's gifts today?

3. Value Your Unique Connection:

- Discuss:

    a) What makes your spouse unique?

    b) What are your spouse's strengths?

    c) How do you best work together when solving problems, making decisions, or creating something new?

    Reflect: How can you leverage this deep connection to enhance your business collaboration?

4. Acknowledge Your Professional Success:

- Share your professional successes and strengths with each other. Include their work ethic, dedication, leadership skills, or any other attributes that make them a valuable partner.

  Reflect: How can these qualities benefit your business partnership?

5. Lean on Shared Belief:

- Remember, your spouse believes in you and your potential. Use this belief as motivation to excel in your business partnership. Trust that you both bring unique strengths to the table!

  Reflect: How can your spouse's belief in your potential empower you to excel in your business partnership?

TEMPERATURE CHECK

Unsure if *Spartners* is for you?

Have you grown apart or are you not quite sure if your partner is actually the best business partner for you today?

Scan this QR Code to access our *Spartners* Readiness Assessment and see if a *Spartner*ship is right for you!

Now, turn the page... we're just getting started!

CHAPTER FOUR
You Are Built for This

The challenges you've faced together and overcome
have made you the best business partners for each other.

Troy's Story: We Stood in Faith, and He Made a Way

After I was let go from the boutique gym where I trained (right after we moved and tripled our expenses), Shantel assured me that we would be fine, and we would get through this. She told me I was über-talented and hardworking, and any organization would be blessed to have me. I looked at Shantel, held her hands firmly, and said, "I will *never* put us in this situation again. I will *never* work for someone else and give them so much power. It may take some time for me to get back on my feet, but I cannot do this again."

We prayed, hugged, and stood in faith. She never told me to find just *any* job, despite our new bills, trying so hard to get pregnant, and the holiday season. She believed in me and trusted that God would work it out. I saw her differently from that very day. I always knew I could trust her, but the way she just took the news, supported me, and overcame the challenge was beautiful. She was tough, in mind and body. She was resilient. She was faithful. She was my partner in not just the good, but the challenge.

Two months passed by, and not only did I rebuild my clientele, but I also catapulted into the content creation business and was invited to work in another small group fitness studio as an independent contractor. It was here that I was later named Class Pass's "Best Fitness Instructor in New York City."

Life is not a movie that you can just fast forward to the end to see how it plays out. One never knows how long it will take or how long they will have to wait before what's next arrives. Thankfully, for us, this season was quick, but more importantly, this season taught me two major things. First: diversify, diversify, diversify! Second: Shantel would be there to hold me down without guilt, fear, or resentment.

Shantel's Story: He Supported My *Crazy*

Troy never let go of the feelings of pure gratitude and relief I gave him when he saw it was okay to figure it out after he was laid off. He was able to return the *favor* when it was my turn to "figure it out" later.

I had wanted to leave my career for years. I never openly admitted this, as I felt compelled to just keep pushing forward, clock in the years, and impact those I could. But the reality was, I had been waiting a long time to leave the school system, as it just did not fill me as I had needed it to.

When I finally left, and we moved to Georgia, I had my chance to do anything in the world and be anyone I wanted to be. I literally considered being a voice actor, vending machine seller, card writer, doula, lactation consultant... the list goes on and on! Although Troy would give me the side eye now and then, he let me figure it out on my terms. He supported my crazy ideas and assured me that he had my back and would never push me to go back to a field I did not feel called to be in at that time. He kept his word, even as moments got tough.

Because I had always been the breadwinner of our family, for me to *not* be in that position was a shock, and it did not feel good. I applied my own pressure to figure it out within specified time constraints, as I needed to contribute to the family. I needed something to do, someone to be. Troy never stopped lifting me up, and he returned the same love and assurance I had once given him. "Take your time. Shantel. We'll figure it out," Troy would say. And that we did!

> *"Patient endurance is what you need now, so that you will continue to do God's will. Then you will receive all that he has promised."*
>
> —HEBREWS 10:36 NLT

Our Thoughts

There is no better partner for you than the one you married. You will go through some crap, to be frank. Whether it be addiction, loss of a child, depression, financial fallout, parenthood, promotion, or hitting the lotto, you will experience moments in your life where you are knocked on your bottom or flown to the top. The way you and your partner work through these changes is critical to the success of your marriage.

You married your partner not only because they are attractive, make you feel good, and share the same interests, but also to work through your challenges together. These are the challenges that will make (or already have made) you the best business partners for each other. This underscores the idea that setbacks and failures are integral to the learning process.

> **DID YOU KNOW?**
> A recent article about how our brains learn from errors explains that the brain is more active during the process of learning from mistakes than it is during routine tasks (Lewis 2023).

* * * * *

You are already a support system for each other.

*He who finds a wife finds a good thing, And obtains favor from the L*ORD*.*

—P ROVERBS 18:22 NKJV

Troy's Story: The Moment I Knew

Shantel has been an ear to my frustration and a shoulder to lean on whenever I feel discouraged and defeated. She's been the voice of reason and the anchor that has kept me rooted whenever my emotions spiraled out of control. Knowing this, you would think we'd have concluded long ago that working together totally made sense. But God does not work like that; He lets it marinate.

I remember it like it was yesterday; I locked in one of my biggest and longest partnerships with a famous outdoor-focused clothing brand. I'm not a perfectionist, but I *am* passionate about my work and always aim to produce quality work. For this campaign, I wanted to create content that pulled on heartstrings. I became frustrated with the shots because they didn't bring out the emotion I wanted, and I needed a break to refocus.

Shantel asked me about my vision, which, in turn, helped me plan what it would look like in my head. We prayed about it and proceeded to shoot the content. She then told me to trust her and let her shoot the shots. She used fresh angles I usually wouldn't use, and the photos were amazing. We were happy; the energy was re-centered, and that emotion showed on camera.

The brand loved the images so much that they repurposed them. At that time, this was huge for me. This was the moment I told myself we should be doing this together full time. Shantel has always been a support system to me, not just personally, but professionally as well.

> *So husbands ought to love their own wives as their own bodies; he who loves his wife loves himself. For no one ever hated his own flesh, but nourishes and cherishes it, just as the Lord does the church.*
>
> —EPHESIANS 5:28-29 NKJV

Shantel's Story: I'm His Rib, and He's My Backbone

When it comes to standing up for myself, for some odd reason, I never could do so in the workplace. Ask my family and friends, and they'll tell you I was super assertive and confrontational even, but at work, that part of me rarely showed up. I was submissive and passive, so far from who I truly was at my core. Forever, Troy would say to me, "Why can't you be this way at work?" or "Bring that same energy there," and then finally, "Babe, I'm tired of hearing about this. If you're not going to address it there, I don't want to hear about here." Troy would also remind me of what I stood for: empowerment and justice. So, he would say, "You are smart; you are strong. Don't let them treat you this way," or "Babe, who do you want Sage to see when he sees you? You are doing this for him."

Though we were in two separate industries, we have supported each other for so long, making each other stronger, our craft better, and our impact wider.

Through these pep talks, tough love, and constant venting, year by year, more and more of my backbones merged together, creating the backbone I eventually used to stand tall and leave my career in 2021. It also helped me foster a more assertive, concise, and professional communication style that makes a greater impact on both the receiver and me.

Troy has always been in my corner, supporting me in being the best professional person I can be. He did not need to have the knowledge of creating behavior plans, accessing student management systems, or creating curriculum (all education skills) to be the support system he's been to me all our time together.

Though we were in two separate industries, we have supported each other for so long, making each other stronger, our craft better, and our impact wider. I would share my presentations with Troy, ask for feedback, and work on how I would engage with people when we were together. He would ask me for caption ideas, to film content, or take photos. We consistently brainstormed ideas with each other, although we knew little about what the other was really doing. We found ways to make time for one another, given our own priorities and work timelines. We were each other's support system.

> *Two are better than one, Because they have a good reward for their labor. For if they fall, one will lift up his companion. But woe to him who is alone when he falls, For he has no one to help him up.*
>
> —ECCLESIASTES 4:9-10 NKJV

* * * * *

A Spartners' Story:

Justin and April Moore (*social media creators*)

Spartners Justin and April Moore (social media creators), didn't begin their marriage with the idea of working with each other professionally.

Rather, it naturally happened as they supported each other in their various individual endeavors. Justin agreed it was best for April to quit her teaching and serving jobs to focus full time on YouTube (while he was still working his 9-5). They both saw it as a massive opportunity with uncapped income potential. While this was a major risk for them, it was also a huge vote of confidence for April.

Meanwhile, Justin had many "harebrained" ideas about how to make money over the years (e.g., he was an art broker for a few years), and April stood by him through them all. She always believed in him regardless of how crazy his ideas sounded and thus, he cherishes that forever.

Together, they have been able to thrive in both their marriage and their business—their *Spartner*ship.

> **DID YOU KNOW?**
> Research shows that family-run businesses comprise 64% of the U.S. gross domestic product (Pickard-Whitehead 2017), and husband and wife teams run 1.4 million businesses nationwide (Orozova 2016).

Our Thoughts

We are sure you, too, have worked together (in some way) for longer than you think. Do you review reports or receipts for your spouse? Do you edit or analyze them, and give them back within 24 hours with corrections because you're aware of the deadline they have? Have you role-played with your spouse on how a situation could go down? Do you listen to your partner vent and offer feedback? Do you help your partner get the job done when they are sick or physically cannot do what they need to do? Have you reviewed their business numbers to make sure they looked okay?

Do you cover for them in their business when they can't show up? Do you assist in creating content for them?

The scope of how you already work together can be as small as listening to your partner and offering feedback to physically being by their side on the first day *their* business opens (after you both spent all night preparing for it). You have been at this for a lot longer than you may give yourself credit. Give yourselves a high five! You are closer to becoming *Spartner*s than you think.

Now the man and his wife were both naked, but they felt no shame.

—GENESIS 2:25 NLT

---

* * * * *

You've seen them at their worst. You know them the best.

Many waters cannot quench love, Nor can the floods drown it. If a man would give for love All the wealth of his house, It would be utterly despised.

—SONG OF SOLOMON 8:7 NKJV

Troy's Story: At My Worst, She *Learned* Me Best

Shantel has seen me spiral through a bunch of ups and downs over the past few years. I was entering my peak performance with fitness, and I felt like a rockstar right before the COVID-19 pandemic hit. I was recognized as the best fitness instructor in NYC for 2019, and I finally had a flow, balancing work and parenting as a stay-at-home dad. Once the pandemic hit, though, everything changed. Now working from home, being a full-time parent, and trying to navigate both worlds felt overwhelming and weighed on me mentally and physically. This weight I carried was not only felt, but it soon became seen. I began to gain weight, first a few pounds here, then a little tightness there, and then all of a sudden, the scale showed me a number I hadn't seen in a long time. I gained 20 pounds over the course of two years. As a member of the fitness and wellness industry, my weight gain really messed with my mental health. It was March 2022, right before my 40th birthday, and I was so unhappy.

One day, I remember trying on a favorite shirt—left arm, right arm, over the head, then over the stomach. This shirt did not fit at all. I dropped to my knees, feeling so defeated. I placed my palms over my face and broke down. I was the guy who had lost 100 pounds... the guy who won "Best Fitness Instructor in NYC...," the guy who always led by example. Yet, there I was, on the floor, crying into my hands with a shirt on that felt like it was cutting off my circulation.

My shirt not fitting was my last straw. Shantel heard me crying, ran into the bathroom, and found me on the floor sulking in self-pity. She immediately asked me, "What's wrong?" She sat down beside me and threw her arms around me. I could barely speak. She said, "Take it easy on yourself. Give yourself grace." Then she reminded me of all

> **Felt compelled to hold it all together for as long as I could because of my own need to be strong, confident, and her rock.**

the sacrifices I had made and the ways I stepped up for our family, forcing me to see the silver lining. She didn't shame me or make me feel bad, and no matter how I felt about myself, she didn't make me feel any less loved. She leaned in and comforted me. Later that evening, we created a plan together to get me back on track with my weight, which included moving daily, more balanced nutrition, and journaling.

There were several significant life events that shifted my focus over those two years. All the emotions, self-doubt, and insecurity put me back into a space I had crawled out of years ago. I knew I could trust Shantel with this but **felt compelled to hold it all together for as long as I could because of my own need to be strong, confident, and her rock**. It had to come out eventually, as all things do, and when I was ready, she was there for it all. Shantel is my closest friend, and the person I trust the most. She saw me at my worst, and through those moments, she *learned* me best.

Closing Thoughts

A beauty of marriage is that you have most likely seen your spouse at their worst, and you know them the best. Maybe you've suffered from addiction and your spouse didn't give up on you. Maybe you were diagnosed with an illness and wanted to throw in the towel, but your spouse stayed by your side and forced you to fight. Perhaps you had a moment of weakness, and infidelity made its way into your marriage, but your spouse said, "Let's go to therapy and work through this." In these moments, you were able to *learn* your spouse in a way they may have never known themselves, and *they are learning you*. You *learn* each other so well in these moments of adversity that, over time, can lead to you knowing each other best.

Whatever it is, you have most likely seen each other through some of the most traumatic experiences life can throw at someone. More than likely, you are better for it. In business, you are going to have things come at you from all directions. Being an entrepreneur is not easy, but neither is marriage. So, if you can support someone through loss of a job or loved one, illness, infidelity, addiction, or *fill in the blank*, you can most certainly get through any challenge your business may throw at you! This is a pillar of a successful business partnership.

Seeing your spouse at their worst means you know their bandwidth. You generally know when they are overwhelmed, when they bite off more than they can chew, or when they are frustrated. Because you know them so well, you can sense when they are tense or need space. This is a great superpower when going into business together because you can step in to support each other as needed to ease their stress. This will ultimately help you be more efficient and productive.

Simply put, knowing your spouse in these ways puts you both at an advantage as business partners.

Even simpler, it also puts you at an advantage to continue strengthening your marriage.

> *Let love and faithfulness never leave you; bind them around your neck, write them on the tablet of your heart. Then you will win favor and a good name in the sight of God and man.*
>
> —PROVERBS 3:3-4 NIV

Discover the Value in Your Spouse as a Business Partner...

In the dark times.

Most relationships have weathered storms they were unsure they were going to get through. The beauty of these experiences is the favor God has put on your relationship and the lessons learned.

Complete the exercise below to help you discover your spouse's value as a business partner in the darkest times.

STEP ONE: Reflect on Shared Experiences

1. Take a moment to think about the challenging moments you and your spouse have faced together.
2. Consider how these experiences have shaped your relationship and what you've learned about each other during your marriage.
3. Record the specific strategies that worked well when working through your challenges in marriage, i.e., "We allowed each person to speak their piece without interruption."
4. Now, consider how these experiences have shaped your relationship in your business.
5. Discuss how you can apply the strategies from marriage (#3) to your business (#4) to help build your own system for working together through the dark times in your *Spartner*ship.

STEP TWO: Communicate and Respond

1. Discuss with your spouse how you can better support each other in both personal and business matters. Share your concerns, challenges, and goals. *Remember*, stay in the **HOV** lane!
2. Show Empathy: Try to understand your spouse's feelings, needs, and limits. Ask questions and put yourself in their shoes.

3. Pay attention to your spouse's body language, nonverbal cues, and cadence/tone when they share. Recognize when they might be overwhelmed and offer support or space as required.

STEP THREE: Grow

1. Thank your spouse for their support and understanding. Small acts of appreciation can go a long way in strengthening your bond.
2. Plan to discuss the items listed above during your check-in meeting times (we'll discuss this more later). Consistently discussing these questions will help you better understand your spouse.
3. Schedule a marriage retreat/getaway as an investment in your relationship. This will help nurture your relationship as a foundation for both personal and professional growth.

CHAPTER FIVE
Iron Sharpens Iron

Working together does not mean giving up all of you; rather, it strengthens both of you.

Shantel's Story: Not Another Statistic

I swore I would never be another statistic added to the number of "women who leave their careers to raise their children and support their husband's careers" list. If this is the move God calls you to, great! But it wasn't for me, or so I thought. I was independent, career-driven, an Ivy league graduate no less! I always knew what I wanted (security and safety), but I was never truly certain if the career I chose was the right path to get there. Still, I was great at what I did. A student by night and a leader by day, I consistently challenged myself, academically, to learn more about my craft of teaching and leading, so I could truly make a difference.

When I finally took the leap of faith to leave my career, I didn't already have something lined up. I mean, that was the plan, but that's not how it went down. As a mama of a newborn, I was totally present with my babe, but I was also vigilant to explore my passions, interests, hobbies, and purpose. I prayed, read, and even went back to the *SoulCollage* vision board I created with a great friend for inspiration. I wanted to ensure whatever my next venture was included all of me. It was important to me to ensure all my strengths, talents, and interests were somehow used.

Somehow, everything I've done, learned, and became would intersect with each other and lead to the beautiful next thing... but what was it? What was *my* assignment? What was it that *I* was called to do? It had to be something that brought joy; I was sure of that. It had to be something that filled my cup; I was certain. It had to be something that would make a great impact; I was positive.

It wasn't long before I began to see how my strengths, talents, and interests (my gifts) kept coming up in my work with Troy. I was able to use my analytical mind to craft awesome packages for brands; my studious mind to take notes and apply them while going through Justin Moore's *Brand Deal Wizard* content creator course; my creative mind while designing scripts, angles, and stories to bring our content to life; and my video production skills when editing our work. I was able to utilize my writing skills while crafting captions, my communication skills when working with brands, and my leadership skills while working alongside Troy. I even had opportunities to demonstrate my acting skills when featured in various videos. Once Troy and I really got rolling, I continued to help elevate our business and saw even more of me appear, thus making our team, OUR business, all the stronger. I was always very crafty at creating visual representations to summarize an experience, and I had the ability to think outside the box when creating new ideas. These skills came in handy when working to sustain relationships with brands and were well received.

When Troy and I joined together, we got so much stronger as we were able to feed our strengths. With me as his *Spartner*, he could release some of the work he did to me so he could focus on those things he was great at doing. He could make new connections and build relationships with brands. Troy was excellent at researching the best brands and contacts for us to partner with, and he negotiated and reviewed contracts with a finer eye. He was able to refine his speaking skills for keynote speaking as well as learn and practice how to use different cameras and apps, etc. Together, like any team, we worked best by using our strengths and in return, WE both grew stronger, as did the quality of our business.

I swore I would never be another statistic to add to that list mentioned above. Today, I sit here proud to have made that choice and follow where God was directing me to go. Troy was getting OUR career ready for US. It was never his. Rather, it was His.

> *And we know that God causes everything to work together for the good of those who love God and are called according to his purpose for them.*
>
> —ROMANS 8:28 NLT

Our Thoughts

How many times have you said to yourself, "I will never…?" Well, we have said it a few times too many. In order to truly live out your calling and purpose, you need to be psychologically and spiritually open to *all* possibilities. God can call upon you to do things you never once thought or imagined you were qualified to do.

We never thought we would be doing what we are doing today, and we're not talking about content creation. We never thought we would be offering or teaching about a new way to elevate marriages. There are so many *Spartner*s who have that same testimony and are thinking, "I never thought we'd be doing this." And yet, here we all are. Be open and *never* count anything out. You (and your *Spartner*) will only draw in closer to each other and your purpose.

For we are God's handiwork, created in Christ Jesus to do good works, which God prepared in advance for us to do.

—EPHESIANS 2:10 NIV

* * * * *

A Spartners' Story:

Veronica Güity shares her thoughts:

"Sometimes in marriage, you find you are a part of your spouse's dream. That doesn't mean you have to let your own dream go. I'm not letting go of 'Mom's Make it Work' (Veronica's independent project). I had to come to peace that it wasn't the season for it.

> **Sometimes in marriage, you find you are a part of your spouse's dream. That doesn't mean you have to let your own dream go.**

I don't think it's by coincidence that God put this idea into me. That is a part of me, and I will not let it go. He is also telling us that right now it's time to support what Wes is doing. At the right time, I will come back to 'Moms Make it Work,' and it will be right where it needs to be.

As *Spartner*s, it may not be your dream exactly, but because you see the passion your partner has, God will give you that same passion to be on the same page and it can catapult you to the next thing. And then, it will be my turn when Wes will be there to support me."

—Veronica Güity,
Grace & Lamb

SPARTNERS

You can make many plans, but the LORD's purpose will prevail.

—PROVERBS 19:21 NLT

Our Story: Leveraging Our Strengths

Shared by Troy

We are the best-matched opposites. Shantel materializes my ideas and creation, while I encourage her to go more with the flow and not over-analyze every detail. Together, we balance each other's temperaments (definitely have our moments when we don't) and spark each other's creativity. We are both strong-minded leaders who like things done in certain ways.

One of us is very tidy and needs everything to be in a specific order (not mentioning any names), while the other will spend countless hours creating lists, schedules, and outlines to process and ensure all the fine details and plans are met. One is very outspoken and can fill the room with laughter and joy within moments, while the other can fill a page with beautifully crafted words to express feelings, describe moments, and get a point across within the same amount of time. We feed off each other's energy, we balance each other's energy, and we can shift each other's energy given the particular day. Together, we create the *yin-yang* in marriage, and we find we create the same *yin-yang* in work.

Once Shantel got on board with content creation and learned more about this buzzing business, she became very knowledgeable and found great ways to use the strategies she learned to pitch and seal deals. This had always been my forte. I was the one who caught the fish, and Shantel was the one who helped prepare it. Now, we could both catch fish, doubling our potential earnings. We began to ebb and flow with our work, where both our strengths were used, and our interests tapped. Here's what a typical deal transformed into:

- We both find interesting brands and share them with each other for pitch approval. (We both enjoy research and learning.)
- Troy sends Shantel requests from brands looking to partner with them for her thoughts on the brand. (We work in alignment with each other and will not work with a brand the other does not agree with.)
- Shantel writes compelling cold pitches for new brands they find and agree to and will draft package deals to the brands who move forward. (She finds joy in creating ideas and analyzing how to best bring the message to our audiences.)
- Troy writes the responses to brands who reach out to him directly to learn more about the campaign. (He enjoys building authentic relationships with people.)
- Troy reviews and drafts legal/contract clauses and negotiates as needed. (He has reviewed hundreds of contracts and knows exactly what to look for.)
- We both create concept ideas for the campaign. (We are both creative and enjoy the brainstorming process.)
- Shantel directs most videos and is responsible for captions/narration. She loves to write and has always loved being behind the camera. (*See* "Shantel's Story: It Will All Serve Its Purpose" later in this chapter.)
- Troy directs most stories/static images, as well as is responsible for lighting/audio. (He loves photography and takes pride in using the best equipment. He is also a gifted speaker and can connect with people organically through stories.)
- Shantel typically edits the videos as she directs them, while Troy edits all static images because he is typically the one featured in them.
- Troy reviews all the legalities of the post and ensures everything is included and mentioned as it should be, and he sends it to the

brand for review to be published. (His strength is in the legal world; this bogs Shantel down).

This is how a typical campaign is handled by both of us, where we have the creative control, freedom, and power we set for ourselves in our different fields of expertise and interest. There are parts of our past identities of working alone that we choose not to use in our current work, and there are parts of us that we continue exploring, thriving in, and sharing with the world. We have not lost ourselves, put parts of us away, or stopped the parts we want to continue growing from growing. Rather, we've collectively put our gifts together as a team to sharpen each other, fuel each other, and strengthen each other.

> *As iron sharpens iron, so one person sharpens another.*
>
> —PROVERBS 27:17 NIV

Spartners' Stories

For Wes and Veronica Güity (*Grace & Lamb*), they knew they matched well and that their gifts blended well together. One was more knowledgeable in tech and was detailed oriented, while the other was übercreative and outgoing. "Us coming together always made sense," they share. Veronica knew this early on and was excited to have a partner who could provide not just in the spiritual and home realms, but also in business.

Wes always knew he wanted to be with someone he could do everything with. "Why would you marry someone you don't want to do everything with?" he wondered. Wes made this decision before marriage. He wanted to experience life as a whole person with another whole person, whether it be business, travel, family, etc. "It is a mindset I had prior to marriage, so marrying Veronica just made sense," he says.

*****

Justin and April Moore (*social media creators*) share a similar well-blended match. April values how Justin loves focusing on the business stuff that she really doesn't want to focus on, like emailing brands, following up, getting on briefing calls, completing invoices, etc. "It's so helpful to have a partner who allows me to focus on the creative side of the business, which is what I truly love!" she exclaims.

Justin shares that April is incredibly creative and that it comes so naturally to her (which definitely does NOT come naturally for him). When brands ask her what types of concepts she has in mind for certain campaigns, she's able to think of a bunch right off the top of her head that the brands absolutely DROOL over. He says, "Since my business brain keeps me pretty grounded most of the time, her creativity helps keep my head a little bit in the clouds!"

*****

Julien and Kiersten Saunders' *Spartner*ship (*rich & Regular*) is another testament to the goodness of God's glory when two become one. Julien shares that Kiersten fills in many of the gaps that don't come easily or naturally to him. So, while he was the person that pushed to launch the business, he knew it couldn't reach its full potential if he were the only one doing it. For Kiersten, she is truly amazed at how much Julien can get done in a year. "He's truly one of the hardest working and most well-rounded people I know, and it shows in our business," she says.

*****

Justin and Laura Lagrotta (*Metro Tours*) have quite different and unique backgrounds. Laura is a lawyer and is very book smart. Justin is in sales and marketing and is street smart. Before they had the idea of what they wanted to do, they always knew they would get into business together. Although they had different backgrounds, they saw how they were complementary to each other, and they worked very similarly on different tasks.

Our Thoughts

When you think about your relationship with your spouse and its evolution, can you identify the layers of identity, desires, behaviors and thoughts that have shed, and the new layers of identity, desires, behaviors and thoughts that have formed in their place? In a healthy marriage, where we become one, this process betters us, strengthens us, and certainly increases us. The same is true when working together.

When working together professionally, it is essential that you become one force so you can work more effectively, efficiently, and synergistically. There will be layers of individual identities, desires, behaviors, and thoughts that need to be shed, along with new layers that will be formed for the good of your partnership. Allow this process to happen, as you did in your marriage. It may not have been the easiest to let go of the "old ways," but as your marriage proves, it *was* for the best. It can also be for the best in your work together as long as you unite your gifts so something new can be birthed.

> *Therefore a man shall leave his father and mother and be joined to his wife, and they shall become one flesh.*
>
> —GENESIS 2:24 NKJV

*****

Spark forgotten passions.

Shantel's Story: It Will All Serve Its Purpose.

There was a brand I always wanted to work with, and we had our chance. This type of content wasn't within the usual space for Troy, but it was something totally up my lane of interest. This was going to be my first content deliverable that I would be responsible for from start to finish. I was excited and Troy was eager to see what the final product would be. I staged the production, directed the talent, filmed the angles of organic moments with the product, edited it, added some effects/sound, and it was complete. This content (video) is one of our highest played videos to date.

I forgot how great I was at video production. In elementary school, I had phenomenal performing arts teachers. There's no way I could write my first book and not mention them: Mr. Dobbs, Ms. Hansen, Mr. Amenechi, Mr. Hoffman and Mrs. Evens (may she be smiling above). This crew literally shaped my life. You never know how much influence and impact a teacher can have on you until they do. Yet, with this crew, I always knew the impact.

I would walk into their rooms and smile, feeling like I was right where I was supposed to be. Whether it was dancing with Mr. Dobbs when I was active and put on my "Sasha Fierce" persona, acting with Ms. Hansen when I had the permission to express deep feelings I was too afraid to show in real life, playing an instrument with Mr. Hoffman (I was never that good), or singing my heart out with Ms. Evens to communities near and far—I was right where I belonged.

Among this crew and these experiences was also Mr. Amenechi. He was my video teacher, mentor, and later, my friend. He saw something in me very early, third grade, to be exact. He allowed me to run our weekly news show where I'd interview guests who performed at our school (yeah, my school was awesome). He would allow me to come after school or during lunch to edit the videos we created during the day. He taught me how to do various camera shots and angles, along with effects and sound engineering. Yes, that's right, this was all in elementary school. He ignited a passion within me that continues to show up in various ways since (I initially went to undergrad for TV & Radio Production), but never really had its breakout until now.

Working with Troy as content creators has re-sparked my passion for video production. I absolutely love to be in front of the camera but find so much more pleasure and fulfillment behind it. I forgot that, and I love it. It feels great working with a purpose while doing what I love, what I'm passionate about, and what I'm—yeah, I'll say it—great at doing. I forgot how video production makes me feel. I love it!

Thank you, Mr. Amenechi.

Thank you, Troy.

Thank you, Jesus.

> **DID YOU KNOW?**
> On average, entrepreneurs are happier and healthier than employees. "People who are entrepreneurs own their decisions and take calculated, not crazy risks to accomplish their objectives. They are also doing what they want or perhaps even better, what they love" (Schroeder 2022).

Our Thoughts

Shantel never once thought she would leave the career that cost her hundreds of thousands of dollars in school debt, about 15 years of schooling, and 15 years of practice, to become an entrepreneur with her husband. She never wanted to *lose* her identity. Yet, the irony is that this identity she held so close wasn't even something she felt completely herself in. There were actually parts of her identity that were lost, forgotten, and untapped in the *identity* she thought she'd lose.

Yes, she could have started her own business, perhaps, but seeing the value in her spouse as a business partner, not just a support system, allowed her to be the boss she was designed to be with the person she loves the most. It created a life that allowed for quality time together, with both family and community, and aligned with the calling God had placed on our lives. Shantel didn't lose herself; she regained her full self, and thus, we became the strongest we have ever been.

> **Seeing the value in her spouse as a business partner, not just a support system, allowed her to be the boss she was designed to be with the person she loves the most.**

Troy's Story: Nothing Is Wasted

Working with your spouse means you give a lot of yourself, but it doesn't mean giving up all of yourself. Working with Shantel has brought many things full circle for me and has reignited interests in me that I forgot how much I needed. I am naturally a community builder. I enjoy fostering real and meaningful relationships with like-minded people. So, when I sat in one of our favorite workspaces, fired up and full of creativity, and began brainstorming with Shantel about our work together, I knew we had to do something with community building. We talked and talked some more and began to visualize the community we wanted to foster and the type of events we wanted to have.

Ironically, this brainstorming session brought me back to my party promoter and event planner days, something I thought I would not do again. And yet, here it was, showing up as a tool that would help us build the legacy we strive for. Once we laid out all the details and ways we could bring our purpose to life, the term "*Spartners*" emerged, and our mission was set. We would work together to build a community of spouses who value each other as business partners and who are elevating their marriage while they work.

> *After everyone was full, Jesus told his disciples, "Now gather the leftovers, so that nothing is wasted."*
>
> —JOHN 6:12 NLT

Our Thoughts

Nothing is wasted. The interests and hobbies you had as a child or young adult were not for nothing. Sure, life happens, bills need to be paid, and doors close. But what made you excited and curious as a child or young adult will most likely still make you excited and curious as an adult. Further, they will be needed to get you to the next level. When you work with your spouse professionally and can truly invest your whole self into what you create, your passions and interests that may have been buried are sure to come out and be needed. And when they do, it is revitalizing.

When you are able to create your business venture with your spouse, you are given permission to tap into all of who you were designed to be. You are given a chance to bring all of you, and the things that excite you at your core will most likely sustain you when challenges and hiccups come your way in business. When you work with your spouse, you are in a safe space to reignite the fire that was once lit inside of you. This bright light will shine in both your business and marriage, thus making them all the better.

Closing Thoughts

Working with your spouse sparks forgotten passions, interests, talents, and possibly even your purpose. Troy didn't realize how much he appreciated his party promoting and event planning days as it built community, one of his most valued treasures. Shantel forgot how much joy she felt producing videos and content. When working together, creating shared goals, and putting our gifts together, we both found that not only were we happier and fuller individually, but we were stronger together, despite the baggage we carried.

Considering working with your spouse as a business partner can be scary. At first glance, you may be one of the many who say, "Heck no! We'd kill each other!" Or perhaps, "Yeah, no. We're totally different." You may even say, "I love what I do... I'm good." You might be afraid of losing yourself or just a part of you. Try to have open communication and be true to who you really are. You can literally be your best work-self with your spouse as your strengths are aligned, interests are respected, and you are equally yoked.

> *Now all glory to God, who is able, through his mighty power at work within us, to accomplish infinitely more than we might ask or think.*
>
> —EPHESIANS 3:20 NLT

Discover the Value in Your Spouse as a Business Partner...

To unify your individuality for totality.

Oneness equals strength. Reflect on the following prompts to help you discover the value in your spouse as a business partner by revealing and removing what's getting in the way of your bond.

Shed Old Identities: Understand that shedding old identities, desires, behaviors, and thoughts can be liberating. Just as in your marriage, letting go of old ways can make room for personal and professional growth.

> *Reflect:* What old identities, desires, behaviors, or thoughts have you consciously shed in your personal and professional life since partnering with your spouse? How has the process of letting go of old ways contributed to your growth, both individually and as a couple?

Reclaim Lost Parts of Self: Working with your spouse professionally can help you rediscover parts of yourself that may have been lost or overlooked. Embrace the opportunity to tap into your true passions and interests.

> *Reflect:* In what ways has working with your spouse allowed you to rediscover parts of yourself that may have been lost or overlooked? How do these aspects align with your true passions and interests?

Invest Your Whole Self: Bring your whole self into your business venture with your spouse. Allow your core passions and interests to shine through in your work, revitalizing both your professional and personal life.

> *Reflect:* How do you bring your whole self into your business venture with your spouse? Consider the ways your core passions and interests manifest in your collaborative work. In what aspects

of your professional and personal life have you experienced revitalization by embracing and expressing your true self?

Unearth Strengths: Recognize the strengths and talents that both you and your spouse bring to the partnership. Align your strengths and interests to create a powerful and balanced team.

> *Reflect:* What strengths and talents do both you and your spouse bring to your partnership? How have you aligned these strengths to create a powerful and balanced team? In what ways do (or can) your combined strengths contribute to the success and effectiveness of your joint professional endeavors?

Respect Individuality: While unity is important, also respect each other's individuality and unique contributions. Your differences can be strengths when combined effectively.

> *Reflect:* How do you and your spouse respect each other's individuality and unique contributions within your marriage or professional partnership? Consider specific instances where your differences have proven to be strengths when effectively combined.

Reignite Your Fire: Reconnect with the excitement and curiosity that once fueled you as a child or young adult. These passions and interests can sustain you and provide a sense of purpose in your professional journey together.

> *Reflect:* What are some moments you've reconnected with the excitement and curiosity that fueled you in your youth? How have these passions and interests sustained you in your journey with your spouse? In what ways can you infuse your work with the enthusiasm and curiosity that initially brought you together?

CHAPTER SIX
Let Go; It's Okay

*We each carry our own baggage and have
our own stuff to work through.*

Shantel's Story: With Time Revealed, You Can Heal

I worked in quite a few different schools and experienced different types and levels of disappointment, frustration, and pain. With each place I went to next, it was only natural to bring some of that baggage with me, similar to how it is in relationships. In one of these places, I experienced the longest, deepest, and most intense level of work-related pain. I'm unsure why I sustained it for as long as I did. I look back and yell at myself, saying, "Speak up! Don't let her speak to you that way! Give it back to her! Whoo... deep breath... don't stress it," etc. For years, I tried to please, bend, befriend, cater to, and support, but it was never received the way I hoped it would be, and my efforts only seemed to make matters worse.

How had all my years in this field brought me to this place of not feeling worthy, doubting my skills, and feeling inadequate? How could I have let this happen? I was a fearless, independent woman... or I usually was, with most people, at least. But what was it? Why did I allow this person to strip me of what I felt so proud and so in control of? Where was I, the real me? In every place I went, people typically embraced me with support, professionalism, and care. I brought that love with me to each new place, hoping to find it again and build on it. I also brought my scars, some of which were far from healed.

Relationships can be this way. A work relationship is no different. I remember learning the term "psychological warfare" as it related to people at work. It is serious and can happen at any job. It's dangerous, painful, and it is *not* okay. There is beauty in it, though. There is beauty in all the pain and brokenness felt and experienced over my years of working with and for the people who hurt me. From it all, I grew stronger and more intentional with my words and actions. I became more empowered to stand up for myself and was ready to lean in to the calling I had been avoiding for years.

Also, I learned many lessons. The biggest lesson was the power of intent versus impact. Without going through what I experienced in various locations, I am pretty sure I would never truly understand this concept. I always have good intentions, but I often found there was something missing between what I wanted to express and how others received it. Whether it was the way I communicated, what came before or after, or what my behavior was like, sometimes my communication had a negative impact on the receiver. Before working with Troy, he brought this to my attention, too. "I don't care what you intended. This is how it makes me feel..." he'd say. This wasn't just an issue at work, but also within our relationship.

> **Even when our past trauma or pain finds its way into our *Spartner*ship, we trust each other to help each other through it**

Many times, we will see ourselves in both the people closest to us (our spouses) and the environments we are in most frequently (our workspace).

When I began working with Troy, I had a lot of healing to do and a lot to resolve internally. I had to let go of the poor teams I had been on and the passive-aggressive behaviors of my colleagues. I needed to resolve the self-doubt I had about my skills and remind myself that I *was* and will always *be* great at anything I do. It was necessary for me to carefully monitor my words and actions to ensure my intentions aligned with their impact.

Now, when I work with Troy, I feel so alive, so powerful, and so... great! What's best is that even when our past trauma or pain finds its way into our *Spartner*ship, we trust each other to help each other through it... like any marriage, business, or partnership should.

> **DID YOU KNOW?**
>
> "Traumatic events deeply challenge people's sense of safety and security in the world. Their confidence in the future may be shaken, the way they understand the meaning of life may be changed, and the way they think and feel about themselves may be different. Relationships can reflect these feelings in a variety of ways" (International Society for Traumatic Stress Studies 2016).

* * * * *

A Spartners' Story:

Julien and Kiersten Saunders (*rich & Regular*)

Julien and Kiersten Saunders' very first conversation about money, while they were dating, led to their first argument, and ultimately a breakup. They learned a lot from that experience. They learned about themselves as individuals, but also about how much baggage they were carrying into their relationship. Although it was painful, they were grateful for the

> **Although it was painful, they were grateful for the experience because it taught them an important lesson about grace.**

experience because it taught them an important lesson about grace. They've since learned to be much more forgiving of one another. They understand that neither of them is perfect, and, on occasion, they may revert to an old way of thinking or behaving. Today, they give each other the grace and wiggle room to grow because they know they will get the same in return.

> *We can rejoice, too, when we run into problems and trials, for we know that they help us develop endurance.*
>
> —ROMANS 5:3 NLT

Our Thoughts

There are lessons and beauty in the baggage and pain you bring into your marriage and work relationships. Before you married your spouse, you may have experienced heartbreak, superficial relationships, or trauma. This could have come from abuse, death, or betrayal, to name a few reasons. While you dated your spouse, this trauma, reservation, and skepticism may have shown up, but you worked through it to put you in a space to be open to love fully again. Still, with all the work you may have done, there are bound to be moments when your pain and trauma come back up in your marriage. Believe it or not, **there is beauty in this *baggage*.** You must acknowledge and confront it so you can evolve through it with your spouse. You will become a fuller, lighter, happier you.

There is beauty in this *baggage*

In the workplace, the same baggage also exists. In one position, you may have been let go after giving your all, and now you are stingy with your time and effort. At the next place, you may no longer trust people, causing you to be emotionally cold and reluctant to let people in. If you have been burned by colleagues before, you may no longer show care or compassion for your current teammates. Experiences like these create baggage that will show up in your next job. Again, there is beauty to be found in that. At some point, you will be called to face it. Whether it be your lack of effort, cold disposition, lack of compassion, or need to be a better team player, you will be called out, and you will need to grow through it.

In your *Spartner*ship, it is critical that you both understand this to truly accept and value the gifts you each bring into your working relationship. We've all been burned, to one degree or another, so together, **you will need to support each other as you work through your pain**. This is essential for you to heal together and be the best *Spartner* for each other, just as you've been the best spouse for each other.

> *Therefore, since we have been made right in God's sight by faith, we have peace with God because of what Jesus Christ our Lord has done for us. Because of our faith, Christ has brought us into this place of undeserved privilege where we now stand, and we confidently and joyfully look forward to sharing God's glory.*
>
> —ROMANS 5:1-2 NLT

LET GO; IT'S OKAY

* * * * *

Check your ego.

Troy's Story: Not Working *for* Me—Working *with* Me

I started this business from the bottom, with people doubting me and not believing in me. As I grew and evolved, so did my business. I built a company and lifestyle brand based on my personal identity. This made it hard to receive feedback; I took critique or advice like a personal attack.

When I first asked Shantel to join forces with me, I honestly only committed halfway. Whenever she would provide insight into areas I felt more knowledgeable about; I brushed her off. One day, I saw a change in her disposition, and her body language read: *uneasy*. After we engaged in an uncomfortable conversation, I reflected and realized I was operating from my ego. Obviously, I loved and respected her and valued her ideas, but I wasn't showing it.

I asked her, "Can we talk?"

With a look full of frustration, a sigh, and then a deep breath, she replied, "Sure."

I got down on one knee, grabbed her hand, and looked her right in the eyes.

I said, "You've been a part of this company for years, from lending an ear for moral support to producing content. You supported us financially when times were hard. You've been a shoulder to cry on whenever I feel slighted, cheated, or undervalued."

Then, with tears in my eyes, I continued. "Shantel, I can't see myself doing this without you, and you deserve an equal seat at the table. You come to the table with a fresh perspective, ideas, and concepts. You have genuinely helped take this company to the next level. By each other's side, this work has far more meaning."

With my knee starting to feel like I was kneeling in lava and my leg falling asleep, I asked, "Will you be my *Spartner*?" (I know, corny.)

With tears in her eyes, she laughed and told me to get up. We hugged, and I promised from that day forward to do my best to *GROUND*[1] my ego at the door!

And yes, she said, "Yes."

---

[1] "GROUND" is an acronym we use to help people work through their negative effects of the ego. We teach how to *GROUND* your ego, so it does not negatively impact your *Spartner*ship. We teach it, and we have committed to live it.

LET GO; IT'S OKAY

GROUND YOUR EGO

GROW
Grow in recognizing, understanding, labeling, and expressing your emotions. There will be times your work, ideas, or even your approach will be attacked. Every "attack" on your work is not an attack on you as a person, rather it may just be negative feedback on your product. Work to grow in your emotions when hearing feedback you do not like.

REFLECT
Reflect inward. Reflect on why you get triggered the way you do, or prompted to do the things that don't necessarily reflect you but your ego. What is it about this trigger that irritates you? When and where does it come up for you? Have you seen it show up in your past?
Reflect on the roots that feed your ego.

OPEN
Open up. When you have an unhealthy ego it typically serves no one. Thus you're closed for building relationships and closed for improvement. To genuinely connect, learn and develop with others, open up.

UNDERSTAND
Understand others. Work to understand who people are, why they are the way they are, and how they come to the decisions they make. This work will help you develop empathy for others and thus understand others.

NOTICE
Notice your surroundings. Read the room. Beside you is someone who also has ideas, feelings and a need to be heard. Many times you may find yourself with all the things to say and not give time for anyone else to be heard. Before grabbing the mic, notice your surroundings.

DROP
Drop your guard. Our guards are built with bias, skewed thoughts, and judgement. Drop it. Stop your ego from taking over and shutting everything else down. Stop playing the narrative you created in your head by dropping the thoughts and feelings that come with it.
Drop your guard.

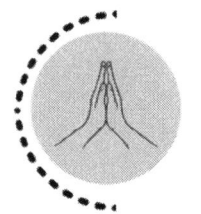

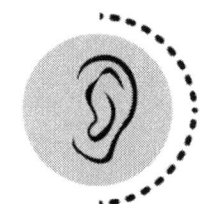

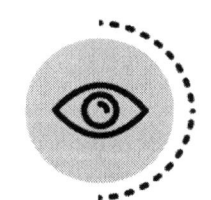

Spartners

Our Story: The Dance

We both have egos; we all have egos; and we all have our own rhythm. In any dance, there is usually a leader who holds the other a bit tighter to help them sway from left to right or step forward or back. When dancing, there's usually the partner who has a little more sass or pizzazz, who may do the extra turn, slide, or worm if they're really feeling it! In a longer, more beautifully crafted dance, you can also see that both partners can dance and lead (in their own way). You watch as the lead is slowly shifted to the other partner, who seemed more reserved, more submissive, and more in the background. Now, you see this once submissive partner as the fierce leader, stunning the audience with moves and an aura saved for special moments.

Yes, we can both *get down* on the dance floor. However, we know chaos can happen if we don't *GROUND* our egos at the door, and we don't allow each other to lead when it's their time, their song, their moment. Like any beautiful dance, we take turns leading and being in the spotlight. Troy, the extrovert in our relationship, naturally leads in our dance and can easily have the spotlight solely on himself. Yet, he knows how much better the dance looks when Shantel, the more reserved partner, has the spotlight on her at moments throughout the dance as well. When the light shines on Shantel, she can magnify its light so much brighter, causing everyone to take notice, watch, and listen.

In our dance, it's not about one serving as the leader and the other just following the lead. It's not about ego-tripping and embarking on a power struggle. Rather, it's about learning when to take the lead, and when to step back without being told, nudged, or glared at.

> *So again I say, each man must love his wife as he loves himself, and the wife must respect her husband.*
> —EPHESIANS 5:33 NLT

Our Thoughts

It is imperative that you acknowledge the existence of your ego and what feeds it and starves it. It is important to address why your ego is what it is and why it shows up when and where it does. Typically, it is our experiences and interactions that create our own self-perception of what we need and deserve, as well as how we allow others to treat us. We each have baggage that has chipped away at our egos and fed them, making them more expansive and potentially self-absorbing. We also each have baggage that has added to and supported our ego, giving us the self-worth that allows us to stand tall.

As we're sure you have seen in your own marriage, your *Spartner*ship is no place to be egotistical, as it can sabotage your productivity. It can impose on your connection and ultimately cause your partner to give up because they feel unheard, unseen, or even powerless. You both come with talent, skill, ideas, passion, and purpose. It is important that you *GROUND* your ego and allow yourself to learn from your partner when it's their time to dance. Together, you will create something beautiful, but you must allow it to happen. That requires being still, at times, and allowing the other to lead.

> *For I know the plans I have for you," says the* LORD.
> *"They are plans for good and not for disaster, to give you a future and a hope.*
>
> —JEREMIAH 29:11 NLT

*****

Be aware of how environmental factors influence your decisions.

Our Story: Impact Over Income

Told by Troy

Parents only want what is best for us. While this is true, we also believe they only know what's best for you as it relates to what they've experienced as good and bad; possible and impossible; or worst and best.

Both of our parents served as significant factors in the decisions we made. Shantel's parents always encouraged her to pursue career fields that were stable and profitable. They celebrated 9-to-5 jobs that provided retirement, benefits, and security. As a result, once Shantel saw that her passion (TV production) would lead to an unstable and potentially unprofitable career, she dropped it and picked up what wouldn't (education). Despite feeling undervalued and disconnected, and ignoring her calls from Christ, she allowed her alluring environmental factors to influence her decision to stay in this "stable" career for 15 years.

My mom also favored the 9-to-5 job that provided stability of income, benefits, and retirement. She, too, encouraged me to pursue a career that would allow me to be financially secure. I would go to her and share the desires of my heart—my entrepreneurial ideas and my risk-taking plans. Though she welcomed them all, she continued to provide guidance that steered me away from my passions and toward a stable job. Unlike Shantel, I did not succumb, but instead used my mother's desire for me to have financial security to motivate me to seek spiritual security and pursue the passion and purpose God had placed in my heart. I did not allow my environmental factors to influence my decisions. Thus, I have been a testament to God's favor and calling, and my mom is so proud.

> **DID YOU KNOW?**
>
> Baby Boomers view the workplace as an extension of their homes, displaying unwavering commitment and loyalty. They tend to stay with a single employer for their entire careers.
>
> Millennials prioritize a positive work experience, seeking environments that foster personal and professional growth. They value flexibility, often changing jobs to find the ideal fit for their preferences (Reaves 2023). Despite being a millennial, if conditioned to think like their parents, millennials can still carry out the work mindset of their parents.

Our Thoughts

In a world with 10 million distractions and a multitude of unsolicited advice and opinions, it is critical to tune out the noise and focus on God's Word. It is normal to seek guidance and advice from loved ones, but you must remember to take it with a grain of salt and put their opinions into perspective. Ask yourself:

- "Are they an expert in that field in which they're giving me their feedback?"
- "Have they taken a risk like mine?"
- "Are they projecting their shortcomings or missed attempts on me?"

Remember, your goals and visions are *yours* and no one else's. Do not get upset when people can't see your vision. Do not allow others to sway you from your mission and distract you from your purpose.

> *Don't copy the behavior and customs of this world, but let God transform you into a new person by changing the way you think. Then you will learn to know God's will for you, which is good and pleasing and perfect.*
>
> —ROMANS 12:2 NLT

Closing Thoughts

It is essential for the success of your progress and overall well-being to be aware of what baggage, history, friends, and even family members you allow into your *Spartner*ship. Of course, they can serve as builders and supporters, but they can also serve as energy drainers and distractions. Just like in marriage, be careful of what and who you allow into your *Spartner*ship.

Your environment can have a major impact on your progress. Your environment is critical to your progress and can both lift you or destroy you. It is important that you keep this in mind within your marriage and *Spartner*ship. Some friends and family can be toxic and unhealthy to your marriage. They may intentionally put temptation around you or "down talk" your union, for example. Likewise, friends and family can be toxic and unhealthy to your *Spartner*ship. They may try to encourage you to doubt your business or distract you from what you are trying to build (with other ventures that do not serve your partnership).

Once you have your protective barrier in place for your *Spartner*ship, you'll need to follow certain practices to succeed as *Spartners*.

Discover the Value in Your Spouse as a Business Partner...

And "Let Go."

In order to truly show up in your marriage and business the way God intended, you should unpack, unlearn, and let go of the beliefs, feelings, and actions that do not serve you or your relationship.

*****

Review the exercise below to help you discover the value in your spouse as a business partner... and let go. Please seek professional care to help you navigate challenges as you deem necessary.

Acknowledge and Confront Baggage:

- Recognize that both you and your spouse bring emotional baggage from experiences into your partnership.
- Understand that facing and working through this baggage together (and with specialized help) can lead to personal and professional growth.
- Create a safe space in your *Spartner*ship to discuss and heal from past pain and trauma. (This step may require the most work based on the vulnerability and transparency that exists within your relationship.)

Support Each Other's Healing:

- Offer emotional support as you both navigate and heal from past wounds.
- Be patient and empathetic when your partner's baggage resurfaces and encourage them in their journey toward healing.
- Understand that healing is an ongoing process and be committed to growing together.
- Celebrate and appreciate seeking professional help.

Be Aware of Your Ego:

- Reflect on your own ego and its triggers. Consider what has fed or starved your ego over time.
- Understand that ego can hinder your partnership's productivity and connection.
- Commit to setting aside ego when necessary and allowing your partner to lead when their strengths are needed.

Embrace Humility:

- Recognize the importance of humility in your *Spartner*ship. Be willing to learn from each other.
- Understand that both of you bring unique talents, skills, and ideas to the table.
- Cultivate a sense of mutual respect and a willingness to collaborate effectively.

Create a Supportive Environment:

- Design an environment that nurtures your *Spartner*ship's growth and success.
- Eliminate toxic elements, whether they be negative relationships, distractions, or temptations.
- Foster a space where you both feel safe, motivated, and inspired to work together toward your shared goals.

Set Boundaries and Protect Your *Spartner*ship:

- Establish clear boundaries to safeguard your *Spartner*ship from external influences that may threaten its harmony.
- Communicate openly about what is acceptable and what is not in terms of involvement from others.
- Prioritize the well-being and unity of your *Spartner*ship above all else.

CHAPTER SEVEN
Lean In

You are only bound to the limits you set for yourselves.

Don't be afraid, for I am with you. Don't be discouraged, for I am your God. I will strengthen you and help you. I will hold you up with my victorious right hand.

—Isaiah 41:10 NLT

Shantel's Story: In Due Season, We Will Reap

For so long, I thought my greatest risk was taking a $20,000 pay cut to co-found a public school in Brooklyn, New York. But when I think about it, I was only 27 years old; I had no children, no boyfriend even, and absolutely no strings attached. Fast forward 10 years later, my greatest risk thus far was not *starting* my school leadership career but *leaving* it!

Working in New York City and Long Island allowed me to empower, equip, and lead fellow colleagues in developing and implementing equitable practices to better support our students. I led fearlessly and passionately and felt grounded in the work I did. I felt needed, and I felt purposeful. Still, I felt like something was missing. So, we moved to Westchester County, New York, where I accepted another new role as assistant principal in a predominantly white suburban school district, where we hoped to raise a family and settle down.

In my tenure there, a lot happened. For example, we birthed our first child, survived working and living as germaphobes through the COVID-19 pandemic, moved to three different homes, got pregnant with our second child, and almost bought a house after a long search during the housing inflation of 2020-2021. During that time, I was also a first-time nursing mama who returned to work under new leadership and relentlessly tried to prove myself. I consistently fought for equity during a cancel culture period, although the army I fought with was small. Between the uncertainty at work coupled with its stress, and the uncertainty of where we were going to live, so much was going on. And yet, there I stood... independent, career-driven, smart, making almost $170,000 a year. Yet deep down, I stood exhausted, disgraced, disappointed, hurt, and oh so... eight months pregnant.

Right before taking the biggest risk of my life, there were many things happening outside of my control and few things happening within it. There were so many thoughts, worries, and feelings swirling around my mind, heart, and gut. One could view what was going on (losing the house we were buying only three days before closing, along with major work-related disappointments) as happening *to* me and as inconveniences. But we saw it as what was happening *for* me, and as opportunities for greatness.

For so long, I tried, pushed, and forced this career. It never felt quite right, whether it be the role, the environment, or the people who surrounded me—but I was good at it. I was making an impact, and I was finding my way with my people. I also had great benefits and one amazing salary. Still, it didn't matter. I had been chasing something for 15 years, and I never felt like I had it. Whether it was feeling valued, having autonomy, or serving with not just purpose, but HIS purpose, it just never felt right.

After we were able to not only find our home in Atlanta, but purchase and close on it within three weeks, it was just another message from God that my time had come to leave both the job and the career. He needed to make my life at work so uncomfortable that I'd be a fool to stay. He needed to make it so easy for us to move forward that He paved the way with grace, love, and no resistance. I believe a valuable lesson for us all to learn is that God will make life so uncomfortable, at times, that we would be fools to stay in the places that do not serve us or align with His will for us.

God will make life so uncomfortable, at times, that we would be fools to stay in the places that do not serve us or align with His will for us.

So, I did what only the fearless, faithful, empowered woman I always was (but hadn't shown) could do... I took the greatest leap of my life... I left my job and my career after:

- earning three degrees and pursing a doctoral degree for four years;
- working for four school districts;
- studying at four universities;
- giving 15 years of service;
- working with and leading 350+ educators; and
- serving 10,000+ students and parents.

I put a lot of time and energy into building my career. Some may think, *what a waste*! Thankfully, nothing is wasted, and I have faith that my training, experiences, and service will all find its way into my life at just the right time.

> *And let us not grow weary of doing good,
> for in due season we will reap, if we do not give up.*
>
> —GALATIANS 6:9 ESV

Our Thoughts

When you hear the term "career-changer," there's so much more to it than changing a job or career. What is really there are the terms "risk" and "risk-taker." It can be easy to grow complacent and comfortable, and just accept the way things are at work for the salary you bring home. It can become easy to just say, "10 more years…" and live each day obligated to do your job as if you're living out a sentence handed to you. For Shantel, though, it was not easy. It was a slow, painful death to her spirit, her purpose, her joy, and even her health.

Shantel will *always* be an educator, but in a career she creates for herself. Her greatest risk of all has led to her greatest growth of all, and with time, it will take her to her greatest success!

We will never grow or know our potential if we do not take risks and lean in.

> **DID YOU KNOW?**
>
> "The average American worker changes jobs 12 times throughout their life, with 65% actively searching for a new job at the average age of 39" (Lindner 2024).

> *Commit to the Lord whatever you do, and he will establish your plans.*
>
> —PROVERBS 16:3 NIV

Troy's Story: Allow God to Guide Your Steps

I remember when I decided to become a personal trainer; I was so excited. This was the first time I had found a way to make money doing something I not only loved, but something that gave me real meaning. I got hooked up with a friend who owned a small boutique gym in Midtown Manhattan. This space was for independent trainers who were already established and had a list of clientele, independent of the support of a big-named gym.

This wasn't the traditional entry point into personal training. Most people who worked at big-named gyms/clubs had their certifications paid for and were then required to work hourly, as they were given clients to train. These clients paid great rates to the gym for training on top of their membership. However, the trainer only took home a small fraction of what the client paid for their direct service. After becoming sick and tired of the inequitable system, trainers frequently leave the big gyms to start their own independent training businesses. They typically look for spaces they can rent out and train their clientele in. This is where I started; I had the space to rent. I could charge whatever I wanted, but I needed the clientele.

I jumped into the deep end and was forced to tread. I was training at the elite level while still a novice. It was intimidating, but I chose not to let the intimidation distract me from the fantastic opportunity presented to me. I was going to be great! I had a ton of clients and relationships in the nightlife/club promotion world, and I knew that if I could make it in NYC as a successful party promoter, I could do this.

To be truly successful in this business, you have to be more than a trainer who knows the lingo, the movements, and the modifications. You also need to communicate effectively, market yourself, and make your clients feel good. I had a positive disposition; I showed up at every session with gratitude, and I listened to my clients. I made them laugh; I challenged them in a way that was tailored to their individual needs, and I always asked how I could make their experience better. This set me apart from other trainers.

Things did not start out easily, and it was okay that I struggled for a bit to find my footing. I started promoting my business on Facebook in 2013 and posted workout videos to encourage others to join. While party promoting, I asked many of my party patrons who showed an interest in fitness to come and train with me. "Work hard, play hard!" was my catchphrase. I started with six clients.

> *"But forget all that—it is nothing compared to what I am going to do. For I am about to do something new. See, I have already begun! Do you not see it? I will make a pathway through the wilderness. I will create rivers in the dry wasteland.*
>
> —ISAIAH 43:18-19 NLT

During this time, my mom asked how things were going, and I told her I was finding my way. She offered to get me a job working with her, where I would have a salary, benefits, and a great retirement plan (environmental factors). I took a breath. *Did she not believe in me?*

A fire grew inside of me at that very moment. My perception of her comment—the thought that she didn't believe in me—could have broken me. After all, I wanted to make her proud, but I chose to use it as fuel. Soon, six clients turned into nine, then 12, and within six months, I had 36 clients in the same space I began as a novice. I was changing lives, making more money than I ever had, and growing better as a trainer daily.

Years later, I realized my mom was just trying to protect me. She, like many of our peers' parents, came from a different generation—a generation that sought out stability over creativity and security over purpose. But I was destined to be an entrepreneur. Taking that job would have been the easier and safer route, but I knew it wasn't for me. When I took my leap of faith, everything else fell into place.

You are bound to the limits you set for yourself. In this time of stepping out into faith, God brought me Shantel. He enhanced my influence in the wellness space. I was featured in *Men's Health, Travel and Leisure, Pop Sugar*, and *Ask Men*, to name a few. He had also blessed me with community. I became a two-time Lululemon ambassador and won "Best Fitness Instructor in NYC 2019."

> **When I took my leap of faith, everything else fell into place.**

* * * * *

Get out of your way. Trust in the Lord. Allow Him to guide your steps.

> *But those who trust in the LORD will find new strength. They will soar high on wings like eagles. They will run and not grow weary. They will walk and not faint.*
>
> —ISAIAH 40:31 NLT

Our Story: Take Risks to Live in Your Purpose

Shared by Troy

As a couple, we embarked on the three most significant risks of our lives during 2021-2022. We always thought we were risk-takers, but we hadn't been challenged to take risks together the way we were during this year. In 2021, we took our first major risk when we left everything we knew and loved in New York to start fresh in metro Atlanta. We left our jobs, family, friends, and culture, and we did it all within six weeks. It took us three weeks to find a house and close on it, followed by three weeks to prepare the house and move into it. We knew we were taking a leap of faith by relocating to metro Atlanta, a place we had never visited or ever once imagined we'd be. Yet, we knew we would be there, hand in hand, as we walked this new path together in God's glory. (We dive deeper into this faith walk with Him in our next chapter.)

Moving to metro Atlanta led us to our next major risk. We home birthed our second son, Phoenix. Despite naysayers and statistics, we felt convicted and determined to lean into our faith and birth our baby at home for the safety of Shantel and the redemption of our spirits. A home birth was never our plan, nor a thought. However, it wasn't until our move that we learned of all the reasons a home birth was best for us, and specifically necessary for Shantel. Within four weeks of moving, our new midwife, two doulas, Shantel's mom, Sage, and I all worked together with Shantel and Jesus to bring Phoenix into this world. It was the most strenuous, exhausting, yet unwavering experience we ever felt. And we did it... together.

Finally, our most recent and most major risk of all was to come together as business partners, *Spartners*, and join forces as one entity under the TB Effect LLC, the "TeamBrooks Effect LLC." There was no guarantee that officially joining forces was going to be successful in our marriage or business. There was no guarantee that we would be blessed enough to continue making the necessary income to maintain bills and upkeep our quality of life. There was no guarantee that *Spartners* was going to take off. The only guarantee we had was that we were in it together, and God was leading the way. What went from Shantel making most of our joint income, to Troy being solely responsible for our income, to both of us working together to make multiple streams of income under the TB Effect (producing media, keynote speaking, writing books, building community, etc.) was a huge risk because so much of it was brand new, and none of it was guaranteed to bring in revenue.

There was the obvious financial risk, of course, and the risk of doing things we felt called to do but were never trained to do. What makes this our greatest risk yet, however, is that we did *not* take this risk to make money, as some risk-takers do. We took this risk to live out our assignment and reach our shared goals: to have autonomy, work with purpose, build a legacy of our own together, and serve the Kingdom of Christ.

> *But seek first the kingdom of God and His righteousness, and all these things shall be added to you.*
>
> —MATTHEW 6:33 NKJV

Our Thoughts

Taking risks (toward your purpose, not wallet) helps prevent loss of passion and enthusiasm and can help you lean into your faith and calling. Regardless of the risks' outcomes, one can find success in them all. Perhaps you stepped into discomfort for the first time, showcased a part of you that has been a secret for so long, or *failed* in your first few attempts. There is resilience interwoven into your fabric when these so-called *failed* outcomes happen. You are also usually better on the other side, as long as you are grateful for the process and can see it that way. Yes, we all fail. But how we fail and what comes from our failure is up to us. One must take a risk to get closer to whom they are destined to become and be okay knowing they will not always get it right.

Without risk, one can be robbed of their full potential for themselves and their service to the world, thus never really living and having the autonomy to be who they are.

DID YOU KNOW?

"Those who believe God will protect them from negative consequences will feel more confident in pursuing potentially dangerous or uncertain activities [like mountain climbing, and social and career-based risks, like moving to a new place to pursue a new job opportunity] because of a perceived safety net." (White, Dean, and Laurin 2021)

I can do all things through Christ who strengthens me.

—PHILIPPIANS 4:13 NKJV

Closing Thoughts

You are only bound by the limits you set on yourselves. You are bound by the negative words you used to label yourselves, the toxic relationships you keep, the destructive behaviors you persist in, and the sabotaging thoughts you tell yourselves.

You can do this. Pray for discernment, listen for His direction, lean into your faith, and trust in God. Do not bind yourself to the limits of the world, rather, live to the heights to which God has called you.

"Before I formed you in the womb I knew you, before you were born I set you apart; I appointed you as a prophet to the nations."

—JEREMIAH 1:5 NIV

Discover the Value in Your Spouse...

And "Lean In."

Leaning into your faith and relying on God while taking risks to pursue your purpose is not for the faint-hearted. It takes a lot of prayer, support, and, at times, calculated strategy. Use the strategies below to help you discover the value in your spouse as a business partner and lean in.

Study Scripture.

>Regularly study relevant scriptures that provide wisdom, encouragement, and guidance for taking risks and pursuing your purpose. For example, meditate on Philippians 4:13 (NKJV), "I can do all things through Christ who strengthens me," as a source of inspiration.

Pray and Meditate.

- Begin and end each day with prayer and meditation.
- Seek guidance and strength from God to navigate the risks and challenges ahead.
- Invite God into your decision-making process and ask for discernment. For example, "Heavenly Father, please reveal the steps I need to take to make this decision clear and the wisdom to discern what you want for me."

Listen for His Direction.

- Take moments of silence to listen for God's direction and guidance.
- Trust your intuition and the nudges you feel in your heart as you pursue your purpose and take calculated risks.

Practice Gratitude.

- Cultivate an attitude of gratitude for the process, even when faced with setbacks or failures.
- Trust that God has a plan, and every experience contributes to your growth and purpose.

Trust in God's Plan.

- Remember that God made you perfectly before you were in the womb, as mentioned in Scripture.
- Trust in His divine plan for your life and have faith that taking risks aligned with your purpose is part of His design for your journey.

Seek Spiritual Guidance.

- Connect with a spiritual mentor, pastor, or counselor who can provide guidance and support as you take risks and lean into your faith.
- Discuss your goals, challenges, and fears with them and seek their insights.

Remember: Every marriage is unique and has been divinely put together to be great.

Reflect: Which strategies can you commit to trying in your marriage?

CHAPTER EIGHT
Reach Your Goals, Together!

More is accomplished when both partners have the same goals.

Our Story: But God!

Shared by Shantel

Let's get into our first major risk—moving to Atlanta.

We always wanted to venture out and live anywhere in the world we set our hearts on. We daydreamed about moving to Santa Barbara and what it would be like to sip wine while looking out over the coast. We fantasized about living in Dubai, where we knew we would thrive and feel a magic we never thought we could experience in the United States. We even talked about moving to beautiful Vancouver, where the water is so blue, the city is bustling, and we would fit right in.

Atlanta never came up as a place to dream about, fantasize about, or move to. It wasn't until a series of unfortunate events began happening to me that I suggested we needed to move to a geographical area that was more inclusive, diverse, and overall, better for us. We loved where we were living in New York, but between home prices (at the peak of housing inflation in spring 2021) and real-life experiences, we knew it wouldn't be home to us for long. It would definitely not be home for our boys.

In the early spring of 2021, we began a deep dive into researching the best places to live across the world for families of color, mixed-race families, and a diverse population. We also searched for places where the quality of life was not at the mercy of the cost of living. Of all the searches we completed, Atlanta and its surrounding suburbs continued to top the list. Atlanta was particularly appealing because 20% of the population were entrepreneurs, just like we would be if we moved, and I left my career. Atlanta then, suddenly, began popping up everywhere for everything. Every show we watched was filmed in Atlanta, and every person we spoke to referenced Atlanta; it just seemed right. So, we proclaimed we were moving to Atlanta. We told family and friends. They all looked at us like we were crazy, and yeah, we were, but we were going to do it!

A few days passed by. The hype, the excitement, and the actions we began taking (researching schools, best neighborhoods and working with a realtor), all settled in fast. It began to hit us—we were actually going to leave my job, and potentially my career, behind. We were going to birth our baby in a city with no other family and no friends. We were going to move into a brand-new place, all by ourselves, and start fresh. This reality hit hard. Perhaps now was not the time. "Let's just find a house here... have our baby here... and we can revisit this in a few years. Reluctantly, we said, "God will make it work," although we both knew He was calling us to leave.

We continued to live our lives that spring as any normal house-hunting and expecting parents with a toddler would during any global pandemic... we stayed inside, searched for homes day and night and continued to tell ourselves that something would work out.

We thought it had when an offer we put on a cute home in Connecticut was accepted that March. It was a beautiful color, intimate on the inside, spacious on the outside, and in a diverse community close to everything and everyone we loved. It was... perfect. The process we went through with our team and sellers was long and dreadful, however. Fast-forwarding to the end, because clearly, we didn't end up in Connecticut; the sellers pulled out of our deal three days before our closing date, June 1, 2021. We were devastated and anxious, but still faithful that God had our back... and He did. It just wasn't in this house.

The night we learned we had no house to move to, we asked God, "What are we going to do?" We had to be out of our current rental house within weeks, and we were almost eight months pregnant. After praying for direction, God spoke to us. He said, "Go to Atlanta." We looked at each other once more. We knew it was time.

There is no such thing as wasted time; this moment was a testament to that! Since we had already completed the necessary tasks that spring (researching where to move, connecting with a realtor, and selecting neighborhoods of interest), the work was finished. Now it was time for us to execute God's plan and **move with faith**.

We had the same goal from the start—to buy a home, raise our family, and be in a community of love, acceptance, and joy for our children. Where that home would be, we left in God's hands.

Troy hopped on a plane two days later to meet with our realtor in metro Atlanta hoping to find a home. He saw about six to seven homes as soon as he landed. That night, our realtor learned of a new home and recommended we put an offer in that night. We were blown away! This home had nearly 30-foot ceilings, was move-in ready, had a beautiful yard, and was within walking distance of a great elementary school. *There was no way we could get that*, we thought. Houses were flying off the market within days, buyers were giving all cash, often $20,000 to $100,000 over asking price, and people were signing with no contingencies. These were deals we could never compete with financially, **but God...**

REACH YOUR GOALS, TOGETHER!

We blindly put in our offer with only $5,000 over the asking price and attached a friendly letter about our family and what we hoped to build in the new home. **We prayed.**

Our offer was accepted four days later, and we closed 21 days after that, on June 25th. Within one month, we were officially homeowners, and God revealed our next step. But then it hit us... we actually had to move. And so... we did.

The House in Connecticut

Our Home in Atlanta.

For where your treasure is, there your heart will be also.

—MATTHEW 6:21 NIV

Our Thoughts

There are many lessons to be learned in marriage and from marriage. Learning how to make shared goals with another person is one of those lessons. In marriage, there will be many decisions made and goals set that require you both to commit. Once you commit to them, everything can fall into place the way it needs to ensure those goals are met. For example, we wanted a house to raise our family in. We wanted to be able to afford it and still love the community we were in. Because these were our goals, we were able to negotiate more, adapt more, and support each other more in fulfilling our end to reach the goals we set. The same can be said when making goals in business.

> **DID YOU KNOW?**
> "Team cooperative goals are extremely important for mutual cooperation among team members...Teams with cooperative goals are more likely to reach time consensus on task scheduling and further stimulate team thriving at work" (Li, Peng, and Liu 2022).

Troy's Story: Schedules Matter

Before working together, we had competing priorities. Shantel needed to get in a workout; I needed to work out. She needed to get her evaluations written; I needed to shoot content. She needed a break; I needed a break. Sage needed a bath; Phoenix needed to nurse. Shantel wanted to go for coffee with a friend; I wanted to get lunch with a friend. Although we were on the same team, our priorities and needs seemed to butt heads continuously. We had to compromise every single day. It honestly became exhausting.

To help us feel as if we each received what we needed individually, we needed to create a schedule. In the next chapter, we will share what a typical day looks like, and we'll talk more about balancing work and marriage later. For now, we'll focus on the importance of creating a schedule for our daily tasks in our calendar. Doing this helped reduce our anxiety and stress in getting things done personally and professionally.

We are both very visual people, so seeing things in front of us is essential. Having a joint calendar was essential. In our past careers, we both lived off our calendars, so creating one together for our work and home was a no-brainer. It gave us structure and the ability to be more effective in our days. We also decided to create a daily task list that included both work and home tasks to which we do our best to adhere. We found having this list gave us the ability to stay structured and helped us ensure our goals were accomplished.

Scheduling tasks and goals looks different for everyone. For us (parents of two small children), life is less predictable, so scheduling our entire week and then adjusting it daily is ideal. At the end of each week, we discuss what we need to do together and what individual tasks we would like to complete in the following week. Then, we work together to build our list. With this list, there is more structure and less compromise, thus we rarely bump heads. This has been great for our *Spartner*ship. This system has also been very helpful when planning dedicated family time and time with friends.

Time is not something we can get back, so making the most of it and being intentional with it should be a top priority for *Spartner*s. When you have the same goals, managing how time is spent is not only easier, but more effective, because you are both working toward the same thing.

"If you fail to plan, you plan to fail," said Benjamin Franklin. Creating a joint calendar and daily task list with your *Spartner* can help hold you accountable and ensure that both your individual goals and business goals are accomplished.

Shantel's Story: I Stopped Trying to "Do Me" and Started Doing US

During the pandemic, Troy gained weight and continued to put on more pounds after we had Phoenix, our second child. Troy working out and feeling his best became a priority for both of us. I was 100 percent okay with scheduling our entire day around him getting in a sufficient workout, as I knew it was what he needed to feel his best and be his best. Beyond that, however, I didn't want his other needs to dictate our day, even though I wasn't "working" or generating income for us (pre-*Spartner*ship). I was still figuring out what I needed for myself, and I knew that I needed equal, or at least some, time to make that happen. I would grow anxious some days waiting for "my turn" to have some time to do *my* work. I even became angry if I didn't get my time because Troy's work got priority because it was *his* work which was paying the bills.

> **Once we officially joined forces, and I stopped trying to "do me" and started doing US... how we spent time totally shifted.**

There were a few months where we followed a schedule that allotted time for me and my personal exploration and discovery. I began a mom and woman blog, started creating user-generated content, and began developing my personal brand. I would spend hours and hours trying to figure out my purpose, praying for guidance, and bumping my head because nothing felt quite right. I would peer over and see Troy playing with our boys, and I would feel uneasy. After waiting years to have this time for my own brand and purpose to take off… why did it feel so wrong? I realized I had conflicting goals—I wanted us to spend a lot of time together and have the autonomy to do what we wanted, but I also wanted to spend a lot of time on self-exploration.

Once we officially joined forces, and I stopped trying to "do me" and started doing US… how we spent time totally shifted. Now instead of me or Troy working alone as the other played with the kids, we'd go on long walks together (as a family), brainstorm ideas, take notes, and create content. Instead of me growing anxious or angry that I didn't have time to put into myself, or the time I put in led me into more confusion, I grew excited and eager to have the time to put into *us*. It just felt right… so right! Yes, we *still* have to schedule our daily tasks for each day, as it helps hold us accountable, but now our day is designed with the same goals in mind, rather than goals that conflict with each other.

Today, we ensure we both have ample quality time together and alone time with Phoenix and Sage. We ensure we both have time to pull our weight of responsibilities toward our work and home, and we ensure we both have time to grow our minds, spirits, and bodies educationally, spiritually, and physically. Working together with the same purpose allows us to have the autonomy we want and build the legacy we dream of. There are fewer competing interests or fights over time. There is no more, "Well, I need to get this done for X, and you have to get this done for Y." It's only, "WE have to get this done for US, and we work together to ensure WE both get it done for the Lord."

> *Work willingly at whatever you do, as though you were working for the Lord rather than for people.*
>
> —COLOSSIANS 3:23 NLT

Our Thoughts

Having structure in your partnership is a win for you both. In any relationship, you want to make sure each other's needs (emotional, physical, spiritual) are met. Although one person may not be bringing in any income, they still deserve the time to ultimately figure out what they want to do and have the time to execute it. Having that time can help that partner explore their interests and ultimately see the value of working together with their spouse.

> **When you and your spouse have the same goals and you work with a shared purpose, it is empowering and revitalizing.**

When you support your partner, it's a win-win for you both. You not only show that you value your partner, but you ultimately support yourself because their energy and actions directly affect you. When you pour into your partner, they will grow stronger for both them and your partnership.

* * * * *

Having the same goals allows you to work with purpose.

Troy's Story: For Purpose. On Purpose.

I think about our dreams, desires, and the life we want to give our kids daily. Shantel and I speak about them as well, to ensure we remain on the same page as we work to reach our goals. We recalibrate as needed in response to where we feel Jesus calls us. While we work toward our goals, innately, we work with an intentional and clear purpose. Similar to when you and your spouse work through child labor together with a purpose to deliver your baby safely, as *Spartners*, you can work together with a purpose to get the job done so your overarching goal is met—have autonomy, build legacy, obtain financial freedom, etc.

When you and your spouse have the same goals and you work with a shared purpose, it is empowering and revitalizing. It can be easy to get lost in nonsense and distractions, but when you can recenter and reground yourself in your purpose, you will be reminded of why you are doing this in the first place, and you'll get back on track to greatness. Doing things "on purpose" matters and will always be more effective than doing things unconsciously, passively, or just to get by.

> **It wasn't until Justin faced the "Grand Theft Paycheck" which inspired him to think outside of the box.**

> **DID YOU KNOW?**
>
> "Discovering your purpose begins with committing to your course." —Oprah Winfrey

*****

A Spartners' Story:

Justin and Laura LaGrotta (*Metro Tours*)

Neither Justin nor Laura LaGrotta thought they had entrepreneurial spirits. Both enjoy the security and comfort of their full-time careers and jobs. It wasn't until Justin faced the "Grand Theft Paycheck" which inspired him to think outside of the box. This launched their idea to start *Metro Tours*, where they could align their like passion for travel with another stream of income.

For them, *Metro Tours* is a hobby. It is not their only income or their lifeline, yet it pays for daycare each month, for which they are satisfied. For them, it's the best of both worlds—it connects them in a different way, while it also allows them to work together without the stress of the instability one stream of income can create. They both have the same goals in mind.

> **DID YOU KNOW?**
>
> "Your work is going to fill a large part of your life, and the only way to be truly satisfied is to do what you believe is great work."
> —Steve Jobs

Our Thoughts

When you and your spouse are aligned and working toward the same goal, it adds real purpose and value to your work. It is an amazing feeling to work with the person you love and trust the most in something you are both passionate about. It is exciting, fruitful, and deepens your connection. We know it's not always going to be roses and rainbows in a *Spartner*ship. It can be hard work, but you will better handle the conflicts that come up because you are both focused on the same goal, thus making it easier to toss your ego and become a better team player.

An added bonus is that this can have a direct carryover into your marriage, as you will be far more resilient and equipped than ever before. Creating goals together and walking through your life with a shared purpose can be binding and liberating for both your professional and personal lives.

REACH YOUR GOALS, TOGETHER!

*****

Having the same goals adds more excitement, care, and gratitude for each other's work.

Again, if two lie together, they keep warm, but how can one keep warm alone?

—ECCLESIASTES 4:11 ESV

Shantel's Story: Side By Side

Before I joined the content creation business with Troy, I remember looking at him nightly, rolling my eyes, and saying… can you just put your phone down? More times than not, he'd say, "I'm in the box" (code for working). You see, I could never tell when Troy was working or when he was scrolling because they looked the same to me.

When I worked, however, it was clear. Papers would be beside me, my laptop out and opened on my lap, and a glass of wine to my left (boy, do I *not* miss those nights). When Troy worked, it was just him and his phone. It could be just him and his phone in the car, at a café, at a bar, at the dining room table, or on the couch, with a glass of wine to his right. To be honest, I only really believed he was working about 50 percent of the time. *I mean, what could he really be doing?*

Now that I'm in the business—WOW—has my perspective, understanding, and appreciation for content creation changed and grown! There is so much work put into planning, designing, shooting, editing, and publishing content… and that doesn't include the creation of the captions, links, and storylines that go with the content you're creating. Also, there is constant back-and-forth dialogue between you and the brand. Whether it be pitching ideas, negotiating rates, reviewing the contract, or sharing feedback and insights, the list goes on. Then, to be truly top-notch, you also send more emails with more content you created to show how great the partnership was. One campaign partnership for one deliverable can literally last months from start to finish. The work is amazing, but very tedious. I had NO IDEA.

Being Troy's *Spartner* in the content creation world has truly opened my eyes to the hard work he's put in. He is no longer alone either because I *now* get it. I no longer give him the *side-eye* when he has his phone in hand. Rather, I ask, "Oh, is that a new offer?" I might inquire about how a video is coming along, or ask, "What does that comment say?"

I get it, and he loves it. We are officially on the same page and we both share an equal appreciation for what the other does because we are both sitting in the same seat... side by side.

Our Thoughts

More is accomplished, experienced, and felt on every level when *Spartner*s have the same goals. Working with your spouse toward the same goals can give you an added appreciation for each other.

- To have someone you love, who understands how you feel and shares in those moments with you in real time... is r***ewarding***.
- To respect each other's work and be able to truly appreciate what each person brings to the table is... ***validating***.
- To support each other and *carry* one another is... ***gratifying***.
- To celebrate the big and small wins together is... ***exciting***.
- To mutually prioritize work life, home life, personal life—all the lives—is... ***empowering.***

REACH YOUR GOALS, TOGETHER!

* * * * *

When you have the same goals, every part of the journey to reach them is shared with your Spartner.

Closing Thoughts

As *Spartner*s, you will accomplish far more when you and your spouse have the same goals. Go slow and go together. Also, do not worry about losing sight of your own personal goals. Rather, focus on growing stronger together for your overall purpose. It will strengthen you.

God has given each of you a gift from his great variety of spiritual gifts. Use them well to serve one another.

—1 PETER 4:10 NLT

Discover the Value in Your Spouse as a Business Partner...

To reach your goals.

Reaching your goals provides profound spiritual and psychological benefits, including gaining a sense of fulfillment, purpose, and well-being. Use the strategies below to help you discover the value in your spouse as a business partner so you can reach your goals.

Be Prayerful.

>Pray about everything. Pray for God to give you the wisdom and discernment to align your goals with His. Ask God to reveal and remove any distraction that comes in the way of reaching your goals.

Have Open and Honest Communication.

>Start by having an open and honest conversation about your individual goals, aspirations, and visions for both your marriage and your business partnership. Discuss what you each value most and what you want to achieve together.

Define Your Shared Goals.

>Identify specific goals to which you both can commit. These goals should align with your values and aspirations as a couple. Be clear and specific about what you want to accomplish together in both your personal and professional lives.

Create a Shared Vision.

> Visualize what success looks like for your shared goals. Paint a clear picture of the desired outcome and discuss how achieving these goals will benefit both of you, personally and professionally.

Develop an Action Plan.

> Break down your shared goals into actionable steps and create a timeline for achieving them. Assign responsibilities and set deadlines to ensure accountability.

Schedule Regular Check-Ins.

> Schedule regular check-in meetings to review your progress, discuss any challenges or obstacles, and adjust your action plan as needed. Communication is key to staying aligned.

Celebrate Milestones.

> Celebrate both small and big wins together. Acknowledge your achievements and express gratitude for each other's contributions in reaching your shared goals.

Stay the Course.

> Remain committed to your goals set and action plan. Challenges will certainly come in the way, but keeping your eyes fixed on Christ will strengthen you through all that comes.

Keep the Bigger Picture in Mind.

> Always remember the bigger picture—the shared purpose and vision that brought you together as *Spartner*s. This shared journey will enhance both your personal and professional lives.

Remember: Every marriage is unique and has been divinely put together to be great.

Reflect: Which strategies can you commit to trying in your marriage?

Action Step:

In order to reach your goals, you must prioritize the time to set your goals, monitor your goals, and reach your goals.

Review your calendars together and designate one hour each week to discuss your personal and professional goals. You can divide the 60 minutes into two 30-minute blocks to help keep balance if needed. You will need to apply structure and strategy to these meetings (we offer tools and strategies in our community), but the biggest step is setting the time to have them!

TEMPERATURE CHECK

Wondering how to actually do this marriage and business life? Scan this QR Code to access our *Spartners Ultimate Guide to Marriage & Business*

CHAPTER NINE

So, How Would This Work?

Let all bitterness and wrath and anger and clamor and slander be put away from you, along with all malice. Be kind to one another, tenderhearted, forgiving one another, as God in Christ forgave you.

—Ephesians 4:31-32 ESV

Communicate.

Our Story

Shared by Shantel

Do you remember those quotes from Chapter One?

"I just need you to listen."

"You're not letting me finish!"

"You always do that, but when I do it, it's a problem."

"I have three kids—our two children and you!"

"That's how you choose to spend your time. That's not my problem."

"That's not what we agreed on."

"Your failure to plan is not my emergency."

"Well, then *you* do it!"

"Your bra has been sitting on this dresser for four days. You've had to open your drawer and close it several times. Why can't you just put it back in the drawer?"

"They are *your* parents."

"Why can't you just place the dish in the dishwasher... not the sink?"

"I love how you move the goalpost when it suits you."

"You spent how much?"

"I need you to understand."

"Talk to me when you're not in your ego."

The fundamental problem that serves as the beat to these issues is communication. Of course, there are other challenges at play: hypocritical behavior, finances, boundaries, time management, etc., but still, with effective communication, even these issues can be deflated and worked through.

Communication is something we both continue to work on every single day. Though our communication skills have dramatically improved, as discussed in Chapter Two, we are still a work in progress. I am still working through my passive-aggression, and Troy is still working through his insensitive feedback. We are still working to allow each other to finish our thoughts before interrupting, as well as not throwing a jab if we feel attacked. We are still working on processing our thoughts in ways that don't confuse or infuriate each other. We are still working to take deep, long (really long) breaths to speak more respectfully versus being impulsive and saying something that only makes the situation worse. We are still working to see each other's perspectives more clearly and be patient in allowing each other to speak our peace. While our communication has become more effective, we are still evolving.

Prior to becoming *Spartners*, we would listen to how we spoke to our colleagues. We watched how we communicated with them in different forums, including those we cared little about. We would say things like, "Why don't you give *me* that much grace?" Or "Wow, if only you could talk to *me* like that, we'd never have problems." We saw that we communicated with those we worked with (and at times barely liked) with more respect, patience, and understanding than with each other. It never quite made sense, besides the politics of being cordial in the workspace. But once we started working together, it became clearer.

When you work with someone, you have signed up (willingly or not) to strive together for the same goal. Therefore, you must push your ego, baggage, disrespect, and impatience to the side to get the job done. So, you listen with more of an open ear, speak slower, if need be, and are more open to new ideas, as this is what you've been tasked with doing. When working with your spouse, this is no different. You're almost instantly forced to shut up and listen, consider their thoughts, and see how they can be integrated into what you were already thinking. You are forced to give them grace when they make a mistake because the work still needs to get done, and you're forced to speak with more patience, clarity, and purpose not to upset them, but to build with them.

Yes, we are still working on the areas mentioned earlier, but wow, has our communication improved through the act of working together?

Know this, my beloved brothers: let every person be quick to hear, slow to speak, slow to anger;

—JAMES 1:19 ESV

Our Thoughts

You may still ask, "Okay, so how do *I* communicate with *my* spouse?" The answer is that you already know *how* to best communicate with *your* spouse better than anyone else. You know what makes them tick, what can break the ice; what they need to hear; how long it finally takes them to get to the point; when to stop talking; when to walk away; when to touch their hand; when to just give them a hug; and when to just sit there and listen. You have been communicating with your spouse 24/7 and have probably reached Malcolm Gladwell's 10,000-hour mark already (Gladwell 2008). That makes you an expert communicator with your spouse!

The harder part is actually applying what you know. You must *care* to communicate with your spouse the way they need you to communicate with them. Think of it as Tony Alessandra and Michael O'Connor's Platinum Rule, "Do unto others as 'they'd' like done unto them" (Alessandra and O'Connor 1998). For example, if you know your spouse needs you to give a disclaimer before you give them feedback, do it (even though you don't require one yourself). Often, we communicate with people the way we like others to communicate with *us*. You may offer humor because that's what helps lighten the mood for you. You may offer long-winded explanations because you require all the details to truly understand something. However, if the person you're speaking to finds humor to be insensitive or prefers concise explanations because otherwise they think you are beating around the bush, then no matter what you say, it may not be heard or well received.

> **You already know *how* to best communicate with *your* spouse better than anyone else.**

For the record, to help your marriage bloom and thrive, you must actively and intentionally work on how you communicate with your spouse (aside from working with them in business). While working with them *does* give an added boost and incentive to really master this, it is essential that it is your priority either way.

> **DID YOU KNOW?**
>
> "Often times people are quick to forget the vows they made on their wedding day. When you stand before God and promise to love, honor and cherish your spouse until death do you part, that should mean something" (Hasty 2016).

* * * * *

Be intentional about how you show up in your home/work/married life.

Troy's Story: We All Have a Choice. Be Intentional.

After a long and productive workday, I remember wanting to unwind and watch TV. Normally I wouldn't eat dinner in front of the television, but on this day, I just wanted to unwind and relax. The kids were down for bed; I poured a nice glass of wine, and I was ready to sit down on the couch and watch my show. Shantel was in a different mental space, however. She wanted to have dinner together at the table so we could discuss our work plan for the week, uninterrupted. We were not on the same page and got into a minor argument about it. Later that night, we talked some more and came to a few realizations.

Shantel wanted to ensure we covered all our bases with our itinerary and didn't want to leave anything open-ended. I needed a minute to unwind and take a breath for myself, so I would be easy to be around. Work and self-love are important needs for both of us, just like our non-negotiables and boundaries are. That night, we needed to be intentional in how we interwove them all together, starting with seeing each other's perspective and setting healthy boundaries to make sure both of our needs were met.

Our Thoughts

In a *Spartner*ship, it can be very easy to blur the home/work lines and that's because... there are **no** distinct lines! Yes, work is work and home life is home life, but when the two are married to each other (literally), you cannot take off one identity for another. You definitely can (and definitely should) create a schedule, though, that maps out when and how you spend your time.

For example:

5:00 a.m. - 6:30 a.m.	Workout, prayer time.
6:30 a.m. - 9:00 a.m.	Family time/get ready for school/work.
9:00 a.m. - 3:00 p.m.	Work time.
3:00 p.m. - 4:30 p.m.	Individual time/pick up from school.
4:30 p.m. - 7:30 p.m.	Family time/dinner time/kids' bedtime.
7:30 p.m. - 9:30 p.m.	Parents' time (marriage check-in, prayer, relaxing).

When you have a *Spartner*, the question of priorities will come up daily. It will be your choice to determine what emails need to be responded to after work hours, just like it will be your choice to squeeze in a *quickie* during work time hours. It will be your choice for what boundaries to draw, as well as who does what around the house. It will be your choice for when to take breaks and your choice for when to keep going with your task. Some of these choices may be a "go with the flow" mindset, while others may be non-negotiable. Make intentional choices to prevent regret, resentment, or repeat offenses in your *Spartner*ship.

And do not be conformed to this world, but be transformed by the renewing of your mind, that you may prove what is that good and acceptable and perfect will of God.

—ROMANS 12:2 NKJV

* * * * *

Maintain Boundaries/Non-negotiables.

Shantel's Story—The Rules of Engagement

Troy and I can be found on the road or walking somewhere during our meetings. At times, people will call us while we are on "work time." In the beginning, Troy would take calls while we were driving to a work location. Although we were *meeting* in the car, reviewing tasks, reading emails, etc., he would still answer the phone. I had to remind him that although he may be driving, we are still on "work time" and I'd appreciate him not taking calls and interrupting our flow. For me, typically the passenger, I wanted Troy to be available so I could ask him questions or brainstorm ideas, and if he was on the phone, I'd have to wait. Because this transit time fell within our "working hours," I didn't want any distractions (outside of what we could control). Troy agreed and has respected that boundary since.

Non-negotiables can be seen a bit differently than boundaries. We see boundaries as a way to help protect our space, but they can be bendable, like lines in the sand, if you let them. On the other hand, non-negotiables are hard and fast rules. My non-negotiable is that I must be active for at least 20 minutes daily before I can actively engage in work. As a result, I rise early to prevent any barrier to that happening. Troy knows I need this and demand this. Thus, he also works to ensure I have the time needed, especially when previous nights were rough. Troy's non-negotiable is that he must work outside for at least some part of his workflow. As a result, I plan for that in our work time together and create work tasks for our car rides, which satisfies both our needs. We set boundaries on how we spend time with our children. For example, there are no devices allowed in one of the playrooms to ensure we are giving

> **It is important to know each other's boundaries**

ourselves fully to our children. To help protect our family time, we've set boundaries for the time of day we respond to or send emails.

We also set non-negotiables for how we engage with work. For example, we don't work with just any brand. We must align philosophically and there needs to be mutual respect. In addition, we have non-negotiables concerning what we're willing to show and do. This is critical not only to the success of our business but our productivity. We save time because we are both on the same page and are not trying to convince each other of why we should or should not work on a campaign. When these situations arise, one of us is usually heard saying, "say less," and we move forward.

Our Thoughts

There is extreme power one can garnish with boundaries and non-negotiables. When you have boundaries, you create spaces that restrict unwanted drama, chaos, or experiences. For example, you may have a boundary in place that you do not work on the weekends because that's your time to unwind and relax. By making this clear to not only those you work with in your 9-to-5 job but also your spouse, you accomplish two things. First, you teach your colleagues not to interrupt you or expect anything from you on the weekends. Second, you also assure your spouse that you are fully present and accessible for non-work-related matters. In this way, your family plans can be made accordingly, knowing that your work will not interfere.

In a *Spartner*ship, the same is true, but goes one step further. In a *Spartner*ship, it is important to know each other's boundaries so you can avoid unintentionally annoying or offending your *Spartner*. As a result, you can work together more productively. For example, perhaps one partner does not want to work on the weekends, but the other does. Further, there is no other time in the week for the two to have non-work-related time together. The couple must discuss and establish boundaries needed to ensure quality time together outside of work. This helps keep romance, intimacy, and love alive.

Creating and setting and then verbally communicating your individual boundaries and non-negotiables with your *Spartner* is critical. It is also critical to create and set some together. These will help you foster and show more respect for one another, and also help your productivity by avoiding conflict that can be prevented.

* * * * *

Share domestic responsibilities.

Troy's Story: Happy House—Happy Spouse

Shantel and I have worked through a variety of shared home responsibility structures over the course of our relationship. When we both worked full time, we had a first-see, must-do approach to maintaining an orderly house. That was followed by weekend clean-up days when we would split the chores and get them done together. When we had our first child and Shantel went back to work, she worked for most of the day, then came home and made dinner on most days. I worked part time and parented Sage for the rest of the day. I also kept the house clean and orderly, did laundry, and kept Sage's room tidy. Once we moved to Atlanta and

Shantel was no longer working (prior to becoming *Spartners*), she picked up the slack I once had since I worked and made our income.

Once we became *Spartners* though, we ensured we had shared and designated responsibilities around the home. Before, it was easy to show favoritism to the person making more money or working longer hours, and not require them to do as much around the house. Now, with us both in the same seat, there was no favoritism. We needed our work and home responsibilities to be equitable and clear. To ensure they were, we split up some chores around the house that we show preference to, i.e., Shantel loves to cook, and I love to mow the lawn; we divide parts of rooms into sections, "her side/my side," and we work together to clean shared spaces and the children's rooms. Of course, there are days or projects when one is more in demand of work than the other, and, on those days, the other picks up the slack. But overall, we have a clear system.

We still struggle in this area, as Shantel is not the tidiest, and our children often make it very difficult to keep the house orderly. Yet, by outlining what we need to do for the order of our home, we are happier, more productive *Spartners*, who both feel appreciated and valued.

Our Thoughts

Having shared responsibilities around the house keeps any home happier and cleaner. Sometimes you may have an arrangement where one works all day outside of the home, and the other stays at home with the kids. You may also have an arrangement where both work outside the home (or work from home) in two separate jobs. In that case, the first one off the clock can start with dinner, as the other folds clothes. For others, work schedules may not matter, and they have gender-specific roles around the house, or there are no clearly defined roles; and whoever sees it cleans it (whatever "it" may be).

Whatever your arrangement is, when working together in a shared business, it is important that there are shared responsibilities around the home. You may be thinking this makes sense for marriage too, which we believe it does. We recognize that every marriage has its own flow, its own dance, including yours! In a *Spartner*ship, however, to help sustain it and keep it (and your marriage) thriving, it is essential that both spouses also team up to take care of home responsibilities. This ensures that there is no resentment built up that is then brought in when it is time to *work*. The goal for us is to have autonomy, and we cannot truly have that if someone feels trapped and like a servant to the other. Both *Spartners* need to truly feel that they have freedom, and thus, both *Spartners* need to help each other reach that.

Reframe how you see the goal of house chores from "it needs to get done" to "when it's done, we get to do... together." It will make the greatest difference not only in your marriage because you're now working as a team, but also in your *Spartner*ship!

> **DID YOU KNOW?**
> "As it turns out, the number of equally shared tasks matters a great deal for both men's and women's relationship quality. Indeed, among recent cohorts, there is evidence to suggest that it matters as much if not more than each partner's overall proportion of housework. For both men and women, the number of equally shared tasks is associated with a greater likelihood of A) feeling their relationship is fair to both partners, B) feeling satisfied with their own housework arrangement, and C) feeling satisfied with the relationship overall" (Carlson 2022).

SO, HOW WOULD THIS WORK?

*****

Learn when to take breaks and keep the romance alive.

Our Story: Work Smart and Play Often

Shared by Troy

Shantel can literally work all day if she is allowed to. She has a very strong work ethic, enjoys seeing things done to completion, and loves the challenge of diving deeply into one task at a time. Troy has a strong work ethic and prefers to work in short spurts. He prefers to work on multiple things at a time, but then needs multiple breaks to move from one thing to another. Troy is also playful and likes to have a good time while working. Shantel loves a good time, but definitely needs to be reminded from time to time to let go, relax, and just chill out. In this marriage, aside from our *Spartner*ship, Troy is typically the partner who ensures they have fun. (Don't get it confused though, once Shantel is in the game, she is IN THE GAME!) Within our *Spartner*ship, Troy plays the same role, and this is vital.

Our Thoughts

There must be someone who either sets the timer to take breaks or throws in the white flag to say "time-out." There must also be someone who ensures work gets done, and it's not all play. One partner is no better or more valuable than the other. The partner who is more about the business will see to it that the work gets done. The partner who checks for breaks will see to it that the romance, intimacy, and adventure stay alive. Both are necessary and should be equally valued.

Keeping the romance alive may ultimately be what you are afraid of losing at the cost of running a business together. We totally get it!

Therefore, in addition to the suggestions already shared, you should also consider the following:

- Give your *Spartner* compliments about the work they complete, as well as compliments about them personally. This boosts morale and self-esteem.
- Have lunch dates when the kids are at school (leave work early and enjoy each other's company). This can keep you connected.
- Do one of the home responsibilities on your *Spartner*'s list. This can make them feel seen.
- Schedule weekly date nights at home. This can help refresh your intimacy.
- Change up your work locations. If you always work at home, try working at a café or lakeside. Changing up locations where you handle most of your business can boost creativity and stimulation, as well as your connection with one another.
- Leave love notes of appreciation and affirmations for one another when it's least expected. This can help make your spouse feel valued.
- Say "I love you," no matter what time of day it is or what you're doing. This is a reminder we all need to hear.

> *"Go and proclaim in the hearing of Jerusalem: "This is what the LORD says: "'I remember the devotion of your youth, how as a bride you loved me and followed me through the wilderness, through a land not sown.*
>
> —JEREMIAH 2:2 NIV

SO, HOW WOULD THIS WORK?

* * * * *

Create Your Vision Together

Troy's Story: Only a Matter of Time

I remember Shantel telling me one day that she felt like she wasn't living out her passions in her job. She shared how she had passions and talents that were not being utilized or tapped into. I asked her what her passions, talents, and interests were and if there was a way she could implement them. She replied that she tried but had little opportunity to do so.

She went on to share that she loved creating, producing videos, and documenting important moments. She enjoyed writing poetry, photography, etc. Despite trying to use these skills and talents within her job, they just never really took off, and Shantel hadn't felt it was meaningful enough. She made great videos to help students and parents understand how to navigate the school under COVID-19 restrictions. She even created the marketing video for the school she had co-founded. Nonetheless, the frequency of doing work like this was minimal, and the impact was minor. She didn't feel as if her full creative potential was being fostered or nurtured.

That day, I knew Shantel definitely would have her passions, talents, and interests fostered by working together with me… some way, somehow. It would just be a matter of time. It was important for her to have shared this with me because it helped her hear and see herself in a way she hadn't before. I felt it was also important that I listened because it was moments like these when I developed more and more desire to have her as my business partner.

SPARTNERS

* * * * *

A Spartners' Story:

Wes and Veronica Güity (*Grace and Lamb*)

Wes and Veronica Güity (*Grace & Lamb*) have prioritized communicating their passions and interests since before marriage. Then, when Veronica spoke about her ideas and vision, Wes would ask her what she would do to get it done. He has the gift of helping her (or anyone) believe that anything you want to do *can* get done.

Throughout their relationship, Veronica always knew Wes to be a person of ambition, with incredible ideas and the ability to lift her up. She felt inspired by sharing with him because she knew he would do all he could in his power to help her see it through.

Our Thoughts

When you can implement your passions and interests into your daily work, you are one step closer to not only reaching your dreams but living in your purpose. If you are going to become *Spartner*s with your spouse, it is critical that you communicate about your passions, interests, and big dreams. This way, you can both work together to obtain them and fill your cups with joy, curiosity, and fuel each day. When you keep these dreams from your *Spartner*, you do a disservice to both you and your business.

Share your passions, interests, and big dreams with your *Spartner*. Put it all out there. When you do this, you will build excitement around your work as well as a strong foundation for your business(es) because you are both equally invested and excited. Furthermore, with God's stamp of approval, you can change lives and do His good work.

SO, HOW WOULD THIS WORK?

* * * * *

Learn your (and your spouse's) workflow and preferences for how to get work done.

Our Story: The Outdoor Office

Shared by Shantel

We kept getting stuck. I needed my device to type; Troy needed to get some Vitamin D to refresh his creativity. After wasting time trying to push each other to work one way over the other, we figured out how to articulate what we needed to

It is critical that you communicate about your passions, interests, and big dreams

work together productively. Troy needed the outdoors, and I needed my devices, so no time was wasted.

This began the creation of our "Outdoor Office" adventures. To meet both our needs and preferences for getting work done, we began going to various locations to work. Whether on a trail where we took notes on our iPhones, or in cafés where we'd have our MacBooks, or restaurants with tacos, margaritas, and an iPad handy (no this is not an Apple ad), we got work done and felt both productive and refreshed. We met awesome people along the way, got our creative juices flowing, and revitalized our energy. We also learned more about our community and surroundings and didn't feel as if we were working too much to enjoy each other's company and the great outdoors.

We each have our needs and we each have our preferences. Marriage doesn't take them away, and neither does working with your spouse. Our Outdoor Office is now what breathes life into our work. It was necessary for us to sit with each other to figure out what the other needed to be productive and feel good. If we hadn't, we would still be trying to fit each other into holes not made for us, and creating an unproductive, unhealthy environment.

Spartners Stories

*Spartner*s Julien and Kiersten Saunders run their business just like any other organized business operation. They have clarity on shared and individual responsibilities. For them, it ensures there are clear boundaries around how and when they collaborate and when they are free to work independently. In addition, they also know what parts of their business will be outsourced so neither of them are frustrated or making mistakes doing something they don't do well.

They also make a point of working in two separate parts of their home. Julien works in the basement and Kiersten works upstairs. When it's time to come together for meetings or lunch, they meet in the middle.

* * * * *

*Spartner*s Justin and April Moore (*rich & REGULAR*) struggle with keeping a work/life balance but love what they do *so* much that, even though they work a lot, it doesn't *feel* like work. Furthermore, in their line of business, there are seasons when they work *a lot*, then others when they can chill for an entire month. They've learned to accept and love the ebb and flow of their work life/home life.

* * * * *

For *Spartner*s Justin and Laura Lagrotta (*Metro Tours*), they work to balance their family, business, and individual full-time jobs. In their household, they work within their interests. Justin cooks and grocery shops, and Laura buys clothes for their boys and bathes them. They run their business in a similar fashion. "Everything gets done between the two of us," they share. There is a mutual understanding of who does what, and they can align their roles to their strengths.

SO, HOW WOULD THIS WORK?

* * * * *

Wes and Güity (*Grace & Lamb*) work together intentionally in both home and work. No matter what it is, they do it with intention: caring for kids, having work meetings, planning family time, etc. They also acknowledge the very truth that, yes, you will get annoyed with your spouse. For them, however, they never get tired of each other. Recognizing the difference is essential to cultivating and sustaining a healthy *Spartner*ship.

> *Every branch in me that does not bear fruit he takes away, and every branch that does bear fruit he prunes, that it may bear more fruit.*
>
> —JOHN 15:2 ESV

Our Thoughts

Instead of trying to figure out what works best for your spouse, ask them. Instead of assuming you already know because you witnessed them work for others for so long (or themselves), just sit down and talk about it. How you prefer to work with your spouse may be very different from what they prefer. You may not even know what you like or prefer until you try it! Be open and transparent with each other about what you like, what you need, and what you hope for. Being around each other for more time than usual can weigh on you. How it weighs, heavy or light, will be up to you. You can choose to make it light and easy by getting it together... together.

Closing Thoughts

It is very possible, and even beautiful, to work with your spouse and keep the IT that brought you together and keeps you together. You both must be intentional in everything you say to each other and do with each other. Your marriage relationship may be the toughest partnership you will ever have. While working together may not come easy, it is definitely something you can do with passion and purpose.

> *Abide in me, and I in you. As the branch cannot bear fruit by itself, unless it abides in the vine, neither can you, unless you abide in me.*
>
> —John 15:4 ESV

Discover the Value in Your Spouse as a Business Partner...

And work together professionally.

Discovering the value in your spouse as a business partner is a prerequisite to actually working with them professionally. Once you're on board, you will need to apply specific strategies to thrive in your marriage.

Review the strategies below, which we recommend to enrich your relationship and create a fruitful marriage. Then reflect after each one and determine how committed you can be to apply that strategy to your relationship.

Communicate Effectively: Leverage your deep understanding of each other's communication styles to convey your thoughts and needs clearly. Apply the Platinum Rule: communicate with your spouse as *they* prefer to be communicated with.

> *Reflect:* On a scale of 1-4, how committed are you to prioritize communicating better with each other?
>
> (1-Not committed at all, 2-Somewhat committed, 3-Committed, 4-Very Committed)

Share Responsibilities: Collaborate on household responsibilities, whether you both work outside the home, one stays home, or any other arrangement. Shared responsibilities contribute to a happier home environment and reduce resentment.

> *Reflect:* On a scale of 1-4, how committed are you?
>
> (1-Not committed at all, 2-Somewhat committed, 3-Committed, 4-Very Committed)

Balance Work and Play: Designated roles for taking breaks and focusing on work tasks, make both partners equally valuable. Whether it be one partner who ensures work gets done while the other maintains breaks for romance, intimacy, and adventure, or both working to keep the balance... prioritize it!

> *Reflect*: On a scale of 1-4, how committed are you to promoting balance with each other for work and play?
>
> (1-Not committed at all, 2-Somewhat committed, 3-Committed, 4-Very Committed)

Be Transparent: Discuss your preferences and needs for working together. Be open and transparent about what you like, what you need, and what you hope to achieve when collaborating.

> *Reflect*: On a scale of 1-4, how committed are you to outlining your work preferences with each other to determine how you can both succeed in working together?
>
> (1-Not committed at all, 2-Somewhat committed, 3-Committed, 4-Very Committed)

Stay Intentional: To work together successfully, be intentional with your actions, ensuring that you maintain the passion and purpose that brought you together in the first place.

> *Reflect*: On a scale of 1-4, how committed are you to staying intentional with your actions with your spouse?
>
> (1-Not committed at all, 2-Somewhat committed, 3-Committed, 4-Very Committed)

CHAPTER TEN

Spartners = Priceless

What is priceless in your life?

"Strive not to be a success, but rather to be of value."

—Albert Einstein

Shantel's Story: Autonomy

I sometimes wondered what life would be like working for myself. How would I get up in the morning and go to bed at night? Would I be a morning bird because I love the stillness of the rising sun, or a night owl because I love the peace of the moonlit sky? Would I go out for breakfast or lunch with a friend, or would I cook more dinners at home because I had more time? Would I look like a diva everywhere I went because I would care about my appearance more, or would I work all day long in sweats and live off coffee? Would I be able to go to my child's school events and be *that* mom at everything, or would we get to school right on time because of juggling everything at home before the day even begins? Would I go for long walks, or would I be on the phone all day talking to other friends who had the freedom to do as they wished?

I sometimes wondered what life would be like working for myself, but I never once wondered or imagined what it would be like working with my husband in our own business and doing things on our terms—not even in my wildest dreams!

Miraculously, here we are! Now, I get up early in the morning, and Troy typically stays up a bit later at night. We eat breakfast at home, and yes; we cook dinner more because we have more time. I don't look like a diva everywhere we go, but Troy makes sure I'm also not running around in sweats every day either. We take turns with drop-off and pickup at our son's school, and we sometimes do it together as a family. We are *those* parents at everything and, yes; we are still late at dropping him off some days. We go for long walks together with our youngest child while we work, talk, and hold on to each other. We pray together and give so much gratitude to God for giving us this life with each other—this life I never imagined.

I was your traditional career-driven woman. I was okay with never being the boss; I made a great assistant, and always enjoyed the freedom that came with that. At the end of the day, I could do what I needed to do. I wasn't held back or held down by strings or people. While I always wanted autonomy, it was always under someone else's parameters, control, or restrictions. I guess that wasn't real autonomy, was it?

Now, I literally make my own schedule, call who I want to call, and do whatever I want to do. I can be with my husband, children, family, and friends when I want to, and more importantly, when I need to. I can say what I truly feel without worrying how it will impact my job security, and I can spend the time I feel is important on projects, people, and things, as it is my call. I can create and protect my work environment daily and never need to worry about feeling so many of the stressors I felt previously. I am free to be all of me. This is autonomy. This is priceless.

> *All praise to God, the Father of our Lord Jesus Christ, who has blessed us with every spiritual blessing in the heavenly realms because we are united with Christ.*
>
> —EPHESIANS 1:3 NLT

Our Thoughts

You and your spouse can have autonomy, too, by building your *Spartner*ship together. When you have a business with your spouse, you create your own rules, your own restrictions, and your own freedoms. Whether it be a part-time or full-time business, when you and your spouse are in the driver's seat, no one can take that power and freedom away from you. With that, you can unlock a future filled with endless possibilities, allowing you to live freely on your own schedule so you can *do more with* more.

* * * * *

We can all be legendary, so why not build a legacy together?

> *"As for this temple you are building, if you follow my decrees, observe my laws and keep all my commands and obey them, I will fulfill through you the promise I gave to David your father.*
>
> —1 KINGS 6:12 NIV

Troy's Story: Legacy

One day, after picking up our son from school, we took our kids out on their two Power Wheels vehicles. On this walk, we were able to discuss personal and business goals while still being present for our kiddos, who were having a ball. After a few laps around, we decided to bring it in to get ready for dinner. I remember pulling into our beautiful subdivision, seeing all the beautiful homes, and watching our kids drive through while the sun was shining. I said to myself, "Man, this is our life." We are both here, present, and providing the life we want for our family. No one is missing out on moments or harboring feelings of frustration, sadness, or resentment. I always want us to be in a position to do this at this level and beyond.

> **Legends die with you, but the legacy lives far *beyond* you.**

We wanted to be more, offer more to the world, and do something much bigger than ourselves. A few years ago, we each wanted to be legends; me in the fitness space and Shantel in the education space. No shame there; it's not bad, but here's the thing: legends die with you, but the legacy lives far *beyond* you.

We realized we didn't want to just be legendary, we wanted to leave a legacy. We wanted to give our children rich cultural experiences that would enrich their lives and shape them into well-rounded, adaptable, and compassionate adults. We wanted to show them autonomy, hustle, and teamwork so they would intrinsically have the ability and desire to seek it for themselves. We wanted to elevate marriages to unthinkable heights and empower spouses to truly use their gifts together to breed new miracles for their families and communities. We wanted to show how great God's love is through the way we love on each other. We work together daily to see this legacy come to fruition.

Working with your spouse can be truly transformational. We are living proof that if you shed the ego and lean into the strongest physical partner you will ever have—the one God blessed you with—you can elevate your marriage and build the legacy you want together.

> *You did not choose me, but I chose you and appointed you that you should go and bear fruit and that your fruit should abide, so that whatever you ask the Father in my name, he may give it to you. These things I command you, so that you will love one another.*
>
> —JOHN 15:16-17 ESV

Discovering the value in your spouse as a business partner is priceless.

Spartners' Thoughts

Both Justin and April Moore absolutely love spending time together. They share, "The fact that we get to work together from home—meet each other for lunch in the dining room, meet up for coffee dates in the afternoon (in the kitchen)—those are moments that wouldn't be possible if one of us worked a traditional job. We will always feel grateful for that!" They find value and gratitude in the quality time they have to work together.

* * * * *

Justin and Laura Lagrotta are grateful for how they leverage their individual strengths and their trust in one another to do their part. Justin appreciates Laura's support in him doing the things he does well without resistance. Similarly, Laura appreciates Justin's money management skills, which have allowed them to take on their new business venture. Together, they are able to make fun memories, and for that, they are forever grateful.

* * * * *

Wes and Veronica Güity are grateful for their *Spartner*ship. Wes shared, "I love having a partner I can be 100 percent honest with and one who is not afraid to push back." Veronica shared, "I can have his gifts right beside me. I don't have to pay for any services... *he* is the service right next to me, with that great mind of his." Together, their *Spartner*ship flourishes because they not only love each other for how they support each other but also for how they grow from each other. As they say, "For us, we went from friends to forever."

* * * * *

Similarly, for Julien and Kiersten Saunders, their gifts are what strengthen them. Kiersten shared, "He pushes me to raise the bar, and though it can be painful in the moment, the result is that he pulls the best out of me." Julien echoed these sentiments and shared, "I need her ideas, perspective, support, and touch to balance out my own strengths." Like marriage, when two become one, they truly complement each other, making each other stronger, sharper, and better.

> *Now to Him who is able to do exceedingly abundantly above all that we ask or think, according to the power that works in us,*
>
> —EPHESIANS 3:20 NKJV

Our Thoughts

Have you considered starting your own business? Have you been working on something for months, or years, but are unsure where to start? There are a lot of great ideas out there waiting to come to life, but an idea that is not backed by action is empty and useless. Don't be the person who thought it but didn't have the heart (or partner) to see it though! Share your ideas with your spouse and explore how you can work together to bring your idea, your legacy, to life.

You deserve it all! When you look into your spouse's eyes or your children's eyes, is there a fire burning inside of you? Is there a will to go the distance to give them the life of their dreams? Most people do what they need to in order to survive and some are okay just getting by. But *Spartners* see things differently and dream big. We want more; we do not settle; we take risks; and we work toward living the life and leaving the legacy our families deserve.

> *Trust in the LORD with all your heart, and do not lean on your own understanding. In all your ways acknowledge him, and he will make straight your paths.*
>
> —PROVERBS 3:5-6 ESV

Closing Thoughts

What can happen when you have more time with each other? You can connect more spiritually, emotionally, mentally, and physically. You can refresh your spirit and energy in things you enjoy doing, and you can rest and relax with one another. Ultimately, when you have more time together, you can work to strengthen your marriage in ways not possible without the time or the intention.

Our call to action to you: Talk to God. Take the risk and bet on each other. Lean into one another and unlock what you are striving for together.

We unlocked a stronger marriage filled with more happiness, better support, stronger intimacy, and unlimited autonomy—all while building the legacy we know God has for us.

You can too!

Discover the Value in Your Spouse as a Business Partner...

It's priceless!

Just in case you missed it, review the list below to see just how discovering the value in your spouse as a business partner is **priceless**:

Autonomy: Collaborating with your spouse in business allows you to establish your own rules, limitations, and freedoms. You become the masters of your destiny, fostering a future filled with limitless opportunities.

Legacy: Don't let great ideas remain dormant. Share your business concepts with your spouse and explore how you can work together to turn these ideas into a reality and build a legacy.

Purpose: *Spartners* are driven by the desire to provide their families with the life of their dreams and calling. They don't settle; they take risks, and they work toward creating a life that leaves a lasting legacy.

Marriage Enrichment: Spending more time with each other enables deeper spiritual, emotional, mental, and physical connections. It provides opportunities to rejuvenate, rest, relax, and strengthen your marriage.

Reflect: In what ways can becoming business partners be priceless for you? How can it positively impact your marriage, business endeavors, family goals, etc.?

CHAPTER ELEVEN
Becoming Spartners

> *Who can find a virtuous wife? For her worth is far above rubies. The heart of her husband safely trusts her; So he will have no lack of gain. She does him good and not evil All the days of her life.*
>
> —PROVERBS 31:10-12 NKJV

You both were called to be fruitful in your marriage, and that doesn't have to end with being devoted to each other or having children. You can also be fruitful in your marriage by working as one in your calling and purpose.

If starting a business was never on your mind, but now you want to learn more, do so by learning more about it with your spouse (and us). If you've started a business and you're now more interested in bringing your spouse on board because you see the value in them as a *Spartner*, give it a go! Use the strategies given throughout this book. Let go and lean in.

Ultimately, when you work with your spouse with strategy and intention and bridge together your unique gifts, you birth innovation and fruitfulness. By becoming one, you produce something that was not here before—that only the two of you can create (even if it is a similar service or product; it is unique to you). When you create something together and it aligns with your calling, you impact your community in ways, again, only the two of you can.

As *Spartner*s we:

- Know that marriage is tough AND know why we married in the first place. We know how we can love, support, and embrace each other deeply.
- Recognize that we've weathered many storms together AND recognize that iron sharpens iron. We will not only survive but *thrive* in our work together if it aligns with the purpose God has set for our partnership.
- Challenge ourselves to let go of our baggage, insecurities, and idols, AND lean into God for deliverance, protection, and provision as we pray for wisdom, discernment, and direction.
- Believe a business partnership can enrich our marriage AND align us with our purpose to be impactful and fruitful.
- See the value in working with our spouse as priceless AND will elevate and enrich our marriage by being intentional in all we do.

In order to be truly successful (in marriage) when working professionally with your spouse, there are many layers that must be addressed and unpacked in order to thrive. *Spartners* are called beyond conventional roles to embrace a shared professional calling. *Spartners* understand the challenges, embracing storms as opportunities for resiliency. Shedding insecurities, seeking guidance from the Lord, and aligning with a shared purpose, they recognize that a business partnership within marriage is a deliberate choice for impact and fruitfulness.

Working with intention elevates their union, creating a legacy only their collaboration can produce. As *Spartners* navigate this dynamic journey, they unveil the profound value of working with their spouse, turning complexity into stepping stones for growth and innovation. May all *Spartners'* paths be those of discovery, resilience, and enduring love, transcending personal and professional boundaries.

Whether the idea of a business partnership was once distant or newly intriguing, the call is clear: explore the possibilities with your life partner. Let go of preconceived notions, lean into strategic synergy, and witness the birth of innovation as unique gifts converge.

Become *Spartners* and join our Collective!

Scan the QR Code below to join our Collective!

ABOUT THE AUTHORS

Troy Brooks and Shantel Brooks (M.Ed.) are a dynamic duo on a journey from New York City to metro-Atlanta on assignment to help married couples who may feel burned out, lack alignment, and are not utilizing their strengths to the fullest move from good to great.

As childhood friends turned spouses and business partners, their leap of faith led to transformative pivots in life, career, and community, fueled by a divine encounter and a commitment to enriching marriages. As parents of two energetic boys, they work to break generational curses and build a strong family foundation by fostering healthy marriages.

Troy and Shantel co-own The TB Effect LLC, a media production company, and have most recently birthed *Spartners*, a framework for spouses to elevate their marriage through working together professionally.

They offer accessible tools, proven strategies, and faith-based principles to help couples not just work well together, but also live abundantly, purposefully, and fruitfully.

Together, Troy and Shantel are excited to spread the gospel about what can be when two truly become one.

REFERENCES

Alessandra, Tony, PhD, and Michael J. O'Connor PhD. 1998. The Platinum Rule: Discover the Four Basic Business Personalities and How They Can Lead You to Success. Hagerstown, MD: Warner Business Books.

Benson, Kyle. 2023. "Emotionally Intelligent Husbands Are Key to a Lasting Marriage." The Gottman Institute (blog) (June 29, 2023). https://www.gottman.com/blog/emotionally-intelligent-husbands-key-lasting-marriage/

Bieber, Christy, JD. 2024. "Revealing Divorce Statistics in 2024." Forbes Advisor (January 8, 2024). https://www.forbes.com/advisor/legal/divorce/divorce-statistics/#:~:text=Lack%20of%20Commitment%20Is%20the%20Most%20Common%20Reason%20for%20Divorce&text=In%20fact%2C%2075%25%20of%20individuals,the%20reason%20for%20their%20divorce.

Brittle, Zach, LMHC. 2020. "Create Shared Meaning." The Gottman Institute (blog) (October 13, 2020). https://www.gottman.com/blog/shared-meaning-is-key-to-a-successful-relationship/.

Carlson, Daniel L. 2022. "Mine and Yours, or Ours: Are All Egalitarian Relationships Equal?" Council on Contemporary Families, Press release (April 25, 2022). https://sites.utexas.edu/contemporaryfamilies/2022/04/25/egalitarian-relationships-brief-report/. Accessed February 1, 2024.

REFERENCCES

Centers for Disease Control and Prevention. 2023. "How Does Social Connectedness Affect Health?" Centers for Disease Control and Prevention: Emotional Well-Being (Last Reviewed: March 30, 2023). https://www.cdc.gov/emotional-wellbeing/social-connectedness/affect-health. Accessed on January 9, 2024.

Drimalla, Shara and BibleProject Team. 2023. "3 Love Stories in the Bible That Help Us Rethink Romance." BibleProject (February 8, 2023). https://bibleproject.com/articles/romantic-relationships-in-the-bible/.

Gladwell, Malcolm. 2008. Outliers: The Story of Success. Boston, MA: Little, Brown and Company.

Hasty, Grant. "Communication is the Key to a Successful Marriage." Renewed Life Christian Counseling Center (December 28, 2016). https://www.rlccc.org/communication-is-the-key-to-a-successful-marriage/.

International Society for Traumatic Stress Studies. 2016. "Trauma and Relationships." Adapted from a fact sheet designed by the National Center for PTSD and edited by the Public Education Committee of the International Society for Traumatic Stress Studies. International Society for Traumatic Stress Studies 2016. https://istss.org/ISTSS_Main/media/Documents/ISTSS_TraumaAndRelationships_FNL.pdf

Laursen, Brett and Christopher Hafen. 2010. Future Directions in the Study of Close Relationships: Conflict is Bad (Except When It's Not). PubMed: Soc Dev. 2010 Nov 1;19(4):858-872. https://doi.org/10.1111/j.1467-9507.2009.00546.x. PMID: 20953335; PMCID: PMC2953261; https://pubmed.ncbi.nlm.nih.gov/20953335/.

Lewis, Richard. 2023. "Mindful Mistakes: How Brains Learn From Errors." NeuroscienceNews.com (November 9, 2023). https://neurosciencenews.com/errorr-learning-brain-25183/.

Li, Mingze, Shuting Peng, and Liwen Liu. 2022. "How Do Team Cooperative Goals Influence Thriving at Work: The Mediating Role of Team Time Consensus" International Journal of Environmental Research and Public Health 19, no. 9: 5431. https://doi.org/10.3390/ijerph19095431

Lindner, Jannik. "Must-Know Career Change Statistics [Latest Report]", Gitnux Marketdata Report 2024 (Updated: December 16, 2023). https://gitnux.org/career-change-statistics/.

Orozova, Maria. 2016. "5 Tips for Working With Your Spouse -- and Making It Work." Entrepreneur (June 24, 2016). https://www.entrepreneur.com/living/5-tips-for-working-with-your-spouse-and-making-it-work/278023.

Pickard-Whitehead, Gabrielle. 2017. "Debunking Myths About Mom and Pop Shops (INFOGRAPHIC)." Small Business Trends (March 29, 2017). https://smallbiztrends.com/2017/03/family-business-statistics.html.

Powell, Alvin. 2018. "When Love and Science Double Date." The Harvard Gazette (February 13, 2018). https://news.harvard.edu/gazette/story/2018/02/scientists-find-a-few-surprises-in-their-study-of-love/. Accessed February 3, 2024.

Reaves, Oswald. 2023. "Millennial Work Ethic: Comparing Millennials vs. Baby Boomers Work Ethic." CultureBot Blog (March 22, 2023). https://getculturebot.com/blog/millennial-work-ethic/#:~:text=Baby%20Boomers%3A%20Work%20Ethics%20a nd%20Values&text=Baby%20Boomers%20often%20view%20the,role%20in%20their%20work%20ethic.

Robinson, Bryan E., Ph.D. 2020. "Wedded to Work: What to Do When Your Partner Puts the Job Before Your Relationship." Psychology Today, The Right Mindset (blog) (October 20, 2020). https://www.psychologytoday.com/us/blog/the-right-mindset/202010/wedded-to-work. Accessed February 7, 2024.

Schroeder, Bernhard. 2022. "Entrepreneurs Are Happier and Healthier Than Employees According to University Research Studies." Forbes (April 1, 2022). https://www.forbes.com/sites/bernhardschroeder/2022/04/01/entrepreneurs-are-happier-and-healthier-than-employees-according-to-university-research-studies/?sh=7453cfe43ee6.

White, Cindel, Chloe Dean, and Kristin Laurin. 2021. "Do Reminders of God Increase Willingness to Take Risks?" PsyArXiv Preprints (December 28, 2021, Last Updated August 29, 2023). https://doi.org/10.31234/osf.io/h74a3

Zetlin, Minda. 2020. "A Supportive Marriage Can Make You a More Successful Entrepreneur. This Study Shows Why." Inc.Com (September 4, 2020). https://www.inc.com/minda-zetlin/marriage-career-success-supportive-spouse-carnegie-mellon-brooke-feeney.html.

Made in the USA
Columbia, SC
18 June 2024